HEALING

AND THE

PRAYER OF FAITH

Third Edition

HEALING
AND THE
PRAYER OF FAITH

Third Edition

DAVID BACHOROSKI

Flowing Streams Books
Colorado Springs, CO

*Dedicated to all who seek to be made whole
in spirit, soul and body.*

TABLE OF CONTENTS

INTRODUCTION

The emphasis of this book is healing in spirit, soul and body.

- "Now may the God of peace himself sanctify you entirely; and may your spirit and soul and body be preserved complete, without blame at the coming of our Lord Jesus Christ." 1 Thessalonians.5:23

Glory is "The manifestation of the presence of God." In this study we desire to see the Divine Presence of God manifested in the local church and in His people.

We will also see the importance of the "Prayer of Faith", what it is and how it works in the church.

- "And the prayer of faith shall save the sick, and the Lord shall raise him up;" James 5:15

In this study, as in any Bible study, it needs to glorify the Lord Jesus Christ. Jesus said:

"When the Helper comes, whom I will send to you from the Father, that is the Spirit of Truth, who proceeds from the Father, He will bear witness of Me, and you will bear witness also." John 15:26-27 NKJV

- "He shall glorify Me; for He shall take of Mine, and shall disclose it to you." John 16:14

We pray that the Holy Spirit will take the things of Christ and show them unto us.

Every passage in the Bible is 100% true. Every passage is not 100% complete, taken by itself. We are not to take passages out of context; we are to rightly divide the word of truth. (2 Timothy 2:15) For instance, "Christ died for all." 2 Corinthians 5:15 This passage is 100% true but not 100% complete. According to Romans 5:17 "We must *receive* His gift of eternal life."

We often think *"If this is true then that can't be true."* By doing this we disallow the completeness of God's word.

Note: If you give me a wrapped Christmas gift, it does me no good unless I receive it and open it. The same is true with God's word, unless you receive it and open it, it does you no good.

The Christian life is not us running around trying to do God's will. It is us allowing God to do His will in and through us. The world needs to see who Christ is through us, His church.

- "He put all things in subjection under His feet, and gave Him as head over all things to the church, which is His body, the fullness of Him who fills all and in all." Ephesians 1:22-23

The body can do nothing without the Head. The Head has chosen to do nothing without the body. Jack Hayford says it this way, "Without Him, we can not. Without us, He will not."

In this study we will try to go into the deeper things of God concerning healing. There are some things in scripture that are veiled or hidden.

- "And even if our gospel is veiled, it is veiled to those who are perishing." 2 Corinthians 4:3

The deep things of God in scripture are not hidden *from* us they are hidden *for* us. To us that are saved they are hidden in such a way that they may be found.

- "I proclaim to you new things from this time, even hidden things which you have not known." Isaiah 48:6

Note: When you hide your children's Easter eggs, you do not hide them so they will never be found, you hide them in such a way that they will be found. The things in scripture are hidden in such a way that they will be found by those who seek Him.

- "And I say to you, ask, and it shall be given to you; seek and you shall find; knock, and it shall be opened to you. For everyone who asks receives; and he who seeks, finds; and to him who knocks, it shall be opened." Luke 11:9-10 KJV

- "*For nothing is hidden, except to be revealed*; nor has anything been secret, but that it should come to light." Mark 4:22

- "How great is Thy goodness, which Thou hast stored up for those who fear Thee, which Thou hast wrought for those who take refuge in Thee, before the sons of men! Thou dost hide them in the secret place of Thy presence from the conspiracies of man; Thou dost keep them secretly in a shelter from the strife of tongues." Psalm 31: 19-20

• "The secret things belong to the Lord our God, but the things revealed belong to us and to our sons forever." Deuteronomy 29:29

• "I will give you the treasures of darkness, and hidden wealth of secret places, in order that you may know that it is I, The Lord, the God of Israel, who calls you by your name." Isaiah 45:3

Our topic is *Healing and the Prayer of Faith*.
It is not sickness and how God can sustain you in it.

There are many good books written on that subject, however, that is not the subject of this study.

• "What shall I render to the Lord for all His benefits toward me? I shall lift up the cup of salvation, and call upon the name of the Lord." Psalm 116:12-13

The best thing we can GIVE to the Lord is to TAKE what He has purchased for us.

The following are some of the myths and excuses why people believe God will not heal them.
"You need to pray hard."
"You never know what God's gonna do."
"God should heal them because they're such good Christians."

"God, if you heal me/them, I will ..." Deal or No Deal.

"They weren't healed because, they didn't believe hard enough."

"God doesn't do that today, that went away with the Apostles.

"They deserve to be healed."

"God is sovereign, if he wanted me well, I'd be well."

"Once a drunk, always a drunk."

"I will pray about the big things, but not about the little things."

"I don't want to bother God with that."

"They can't be healed because they must suffer the consequences of their actions."

"Everybody needs a thorn in the flesh. I guess this is just mine."

"We must be very careful; there are cults and isms out there."

(The fact that there are counterfeits proves that there is a real, you won't see a counterfeit paper bag because it is not worth counterfeiting.)

Most people are not opposed to being healed, they are opposed to God doing it.

In this age of information technology, we sometimes get the idea that knowledge is god and is the answer to everything. In Ephesians 1:17 Paul prayed: "That the God of our Lord Jesus Christ, the Father of glory, may give to you a spirit of wisdom and of revelation in the knowledge of Him." We need more revelation, not more information. To help understand the reality of this statement; How many times did you hear the gospel preached before you believed it? You were given the information many times but until you received the revelation in your heart, they were just words. After you received the revelation of the Lord Jesus Christ the words got into your heart and you became a new creation in Christ Jesus.

Paul continues: "I pray that the eyes of your heart may be enlightened, so that you may know what is the hope of His calling, what are the riches of the glory of His inheritance in the saints, and what is the surpassing greatness of His power toward us who believe." Ephesians 1:18-19

We must be careful that we do not reduce our theology to nothing more than a mental exercise. We need enlightenment in our hearts to see the vast riches of the Lord Jesus Christ. This can only be done by the Spirit of God as He reveals the Lord Jesus Christ to us.

When a father dies, he usually leaves something to his family called an inheritance. When Jesus died, He left an inheritance to the Father. We are that inheritance. We are an inheritance that won't be used up, the Father will enjoy us throughout eternity. Can you imagine, fellow Christian, the joy that you will give the Father for eternity.

Paul prays that we might know, in our hearts. "The surpassing greatness of His power toward us who believe." He doesn't call this power "great", that's not enough. He calls it "surpassing greatness" towards us who believe. May the Lord be gracious to us and give us a revelation of what the Lord Jesus Christ has given to us. Let us not be satisfied with just knowing that I will go to heaven when I die. May we ever seek to know the surpassing greatness of His power towards us who believe. In the study of healing, as in any Bible study, the answer has to point to the person and finished work of the Lord Jesus Christ. If the answer points to anything or anybody else, you know it is pointing to the wrong thing. John Wycliffe expressed it this way; "Any teaching which detracts from the centrality of Christ under the pretense of leading men to maturity and perfection is a perversion that threatens the very essence of the faith."

Atonement means reconciliation of God and humankind for sin. Healing is not automatically in the atonement, but His atonement sure opened the door so we can be healed. You could say salvation is not in the atonement, but His atonement sure opened the door so we can be saved. There can be no other basis for God blessing us other than through the atoning sacrifice of His Son. If all people are automatically healed or saved through His atonement there would be no need to pray for healing or for a person's salvation. We are told to pray for one another so we can be healed. James 5:16 Healing is available to us because of His atoning sacrifice.

We cannot say that every time under every circumstance God will do this or that. We are led by the Spirit as He quickens the word to us and we allow Him to work through us as He chooses. This is what makes the Christian life so exciting.

We should not use these teachings in a legalistic way where we say; God will always work this way or that under every circumstance. Legalism will always lead to a critical spirit. We are led by the Spirit of God not a set of rules and regulations. This book has tools and suggestions to put in your toolbox as led by the Holy Spirit as you seek healing for yourself and as you pray for others. A well-equipped toolbox is more likely to be used than one that isn't. I urge you to allow the love of God to flow through you as you minister healing to yourself and others.

I pray this will be a year of walking with the Lord and allowing Him to give us an ever-increasing revelation of the Lord Jesus Christ.

My prayer is that as you read these words you would be completely healed in spirit, soul and body and you would have a deeper walk with the Lord as you trust in Him and His word.

THE PATH OF GLORY

Glory – (Greek) DOXA – means dignity, glory, honor, praise, worship. It is the root word for doxology. "Praise God from whom all blessings flow. Praise Him all creatures here below, praise Him above ye heavenly hosts, Praise Father, Son and Holy Ghost.

- "Let us make *man* in our image, after our likeness; and let them have dominion over the fish of the sea, and over the fowl of the air, and over the cattle, and over all the earth, and over every creeping thing that creepeth upon the earth." Genesis 1:26

The angels asked; What is man? What is a man? What is a man?

- "When I consider thy heavens, the work of thy fingers, the moon and the stars, which thou hast ordained; what is man, that thou dost take thought of him? And the son of man, that thou dost care for him? Yet thou hast made him a little lower than God, (Elohim), and dost crown him with *Glory* and majesty! Thou dost make him to rule over the works of thy hands; Thou hast put all things under his feet." Psalm 8: 3-6

Elohim is the Hebrew plural word for God. It shows God the Father, God the Son and God the Holy Spirit.

From eternity past the order was (1) The Triune Godhead, (2) Archangels and, (3) Angels. Now there is a new order in creation. (1) The Triune Godhead, (2) Man, (3) Archangels, and (4) Angels.

Note: The lesser worships and serves the greater. Never are we told to worship and serve the angels. We are to worship and serve the Father not the angels. "Are they not all ministering spirits, sent out to render service for the sake of those who will inherit salvation." Hebrews 1:14

"Let no one keep defrauding you of your prize by delighting in self-abasement and the worship of the angels, taking his stand on visions he has seen, inflated without cause by his fleshly mind." Colossians 2:18

Man was crowned with Glory. Man was not crowned with diamonds, gold or rubies. These were things that were destined to perish. Man was crowned with God's Glory! Man was crowned with the Glory of God. The Glory of God is God Himself. Glory is the manifestation of the presence of God.

Satan was dethroned from heaven and cast down to earth.

- "How you have fallen from heaven, O star of the morning, son of the dawn! You have been cut down to the earth, You who have weakened the nations! But you said in your heart, I will ascend to heaven; I will raise my throne above the stars of God, And I will sit on the mount of assembly in the recesses of the north. I will ascend above the heights of the clouds; I will make myself like the Most High." Isaiah 14: 12-14

Satan saw that his power was now being usurped by man. If he could tempt man and get him to disobey God, then man would lose his covering of Glory and his dominion over the earth. If he could defeat man and get him to disobey God he would have forever defeated God. Man was given a free will and could choose to obey or disobey God and he chose to disobey. When Adam sinned, the Glory of God departed.

• "And they heard the voice of the Lord God walking in the garden in the cool of the day: and Adam and his wife hid themselves from the presence of the Lord God amongst the trees of the garden. And the Lord God called unto him, where art thou? And he said, I heard thy voice in the garden, and I was afraid, because I was naked; and I hid myself." Genesis 3: 8-10

The covering of Glory that Adam had was gone. Fear came into his life and he saw that he was naked.

• "For in Adam all die." 1 Corinthians 15:22

• "For all have sinned and come short of the glory of God." Romans 3:23

If you're playing with your kids in the park and one of them falls and hurts himself, your immediate reaction as a parent is to run to the child, hold him in your arms and comfort him. God could not do that. If he would have touched Adam, His Glory would have consumed him. "For our God is a consuming fire." Hebrews 12:29 He consumes sin.

God spoke that man would have dominion over the works of His hands. Psalm 8:6 God's Word will always come to pass, He cannot lie. Here was a dilemma. How could man have dominion over the works of His hands, without the Glory of God? Satan thought he had won, but God had a plan from eternity. He would restore the Glory that was lost.

From all eternity there was a redemption plan for man. There was no redemption plan for the angels that had fallen, so Satan thought that he had won. He thought he had forever defeated God. This is very aptly expressed in the following song written in 1894 by Johnson Oatman, Jr.

Holy, Holy, Is What the Angels Sing

Chorus:
Holy, Holy is what the angels sing,
And I expect to help them make the courts of
    heaven ring.
But when I sing redemptions story, they will fold
    their wings
for angels never felt the joys that our salvation
    brings.

Verse 2
But I hear another anthem, blending voices clear
    and strong,
"Unto Him who has redeemed us and hath
    bought us," is the song;
We have come through tribulation to the land so
    fair and bright,
In the fountain freely flowing He has made our
    garments white.

Verse 3

Then the angels stand and listen for they cannot
    join the song,
Like the sound of many waters, by that happy,
    blood-washed throng,
For they sing about great trials, battles fought
    and vict'ries won,
And they praise their great redeemer, who hath
    said to them, "Well done."

Verse 4

So, although I'm not an angel, yet I know that
    over there
I will join a blessed chorus that the angels cannot
    share;
I will sing about my Savior, who upon dark
    Calvary
Freely pardoned my transgressions, died to set a
    sinner free.

"If Satan had seen the plan, he never would have
encouraged God's spotless lamb to be lifted to the altar
of the cross where His innocent blood could be shed
to cleanse man and to pay the price so once again man
could stand in the Glory of God's presence."

• "But we speak the wisdom of God in a
mystery, even the hidden wisdom, which God
ordained before the world unto our glory; which
none of the princes of this world knew; for had
they known it, they would not have crucified the
Lord of Glory." 1 Corinthians 2:7-8

These things were hidden *for* us, they were not
hidden *from* us.

- "The mystery which has been hidden from the past ages and generations; but has now been manifested to His saints, to whom God willed to make known what is the riches of the glory of this mystery among the gentiles, which is Christ in you, the hope of Glory." Colossians 1: 26-27

- "For it was fitting for Him, for Whom are all things, and through Him are all things, in bringing many sons to glory." Hebrews 2:10

- "But we all, with unveiled face beholding as in a mirror the Glory of the Lord, are being transformed into the same image from glory to glory, just as from the Lord, the Spirit." 2 Corinthians 3:18

"The Father of Glory (Ephesians 1:17), sent the Lord of Glory to lift up man who had been crowned with Glory, but had fallen from Glory, back into the Glory of His presence." Excerpt from *The Blood and the Glory* Author Billye Brim

Salvation is not just what we are saved "From" – the devil and sin.

Salvation is also what we are saved "To" – God and His Glory!

It is the Blood of Jesus that *cleanses* us, and *covers* us, and *enables* us to stand in His Glory.

- "I glorified Thee on the earth, having accomplished the work which Thou hast given me to do. And now, Glorify Thou Me together with Thyself, Father, with the Glory which I ever had with Thee before the world was." John 17: 4-5

• "And the Glory which Thou hast given Me, I have given to them; that they may be one, just as We are one;" John 17:22

• "Father, I desire that they also, whom Thou hast given Me, be with Me where I am, in order that they may behold My Glory, which Thou hast given Me; For Thou didst love Me before the foundation of the world." John 17: 24

• "I pray that the eyes of your heart may be enlightened, so that you may know what is the hope of His calling, what are the riches of the Glory of His inheritance in the saints." Ephesians 1:18

• "Therefore I exhort the elders among you, as your fellow-elder and witness of the sufferings of Christ, and a partaker of the Glory that is to be revealed," 1 Peter 5:1

• "…The Lord Jesus Christ; who will transform the body of our humble state into conformity with the body of His Glory, by the exertion of His power that He has even to subject all things to himself." Philippians 3:20-21

• "When the Chief Shepherd appears, you will receive the unfading crown of Glory." 1 Peter 5:4

When you are caught up in sin you should be concerned about the loss of glory, not the punishment.

A mirror reflects the image. We are not the image, we reflect the image of Christ.

- "But we all, with unveiled face, beholding as in a mirror the Glory of the Lord, are being transformed into the same image from Glory to Glory, just as from the Lord, the Spirit." 2 Corinthians 3:18

Are you reflecting a distorted image of Christ? Look at him, he's the spitting image of his father.

THE GREAT COVENANTS
OF SCRIPTURE

Right now you may be thinking, we're studying the topic of healing and faith. What do the Old Covenants have to do with the topic of healing?

Many New Testament believers try to base their healing on the Old Covenants, they get confused and don't understand their relationship to God based on the New Testament.

The Eight Covenants. Summary:
   (1) The Edenic Covenant (Gen. 2:16) conditions the life of man in innocence.
   (2) The Adamic Covenant (Gen 3:15) conditions the life of fallen man and gives promise of a Redeemer.
   (3) The Noahic Covenant (Gen. 9:16) establishes the principle of human government.
   (4) The Abrahamic Covenant (Gen. 12:2) founds the nation of Israel and confirms, with specific additions, the Adamic promise of redemption.
   (5) The Mosaic Covenant (Ex. 19:5) condemns all men, "for all have sinned" (Rom. 3:23: 5:12)
   (6) The Palestinian Covenant (Dt. 30:3) secures the final restoration and conversion of Israel.
   (7) The David Covenant (2 Sam. 7:16) establishes

the perpetuity of the Davidic family (fulfilled in Christ, Mt. 1:1; Lk. 1:31-33; Rom. 1:3), and of the Davidic kingdom over Israel and over the whole earth, to be fulfilled in and by Christ (2 Sam. 7:8-17; Zech. 12:8; Lk. 1:31-33; Acts 15:14-17; 1 Cor. 15;24). And

(8) And the New Covenant (Heb 8:8) rests upon the sacrifice of Christ and secures the eternal blessedness, under the Abrahamic Covenant (Gal 3:13-29), of all who believe. It is absolutely unconditional and, since no responsibility is by it committed to man, it is final and irreversible." *New Scofield Reference Bible, 1967 by Oxford University Press, Inc.*

The New Covenant, the last of the eight great covenants of Scripture, is

(1) "better" than the Mosaic Covenant (Ex. 19-5), not morally but efficaciously (Heb. 7:19, Rom. 8:3-4).

(2) It is established upon "better" *(unconditional)* promises. In the Mosaic Covenant God said, *"If ye will"* (Ex. 19-5); in the New Covenant He Says, *"I will"* (Heb. 8:10-,12).

(3) Under the Mosaic Covenant obedience sprang from fear (Heb. 2:2, 12:25-27); under the New it issues from a willing heart and mind (Heb. 8:10).

(4) The New Covenant secures the personal revelation of the Lord to every believer (Heb. 8:11).

(5) It assures the complete oblivion of sins (Heb. 8:12; 10:17).

(6) It rests upon an accomplished redemption (Mt. 26:27-28; 1 Cor. 11:25, Heb. 9:11-12, 18-23). Bear in mind that the same Greek word

(diatheke) is rendered both as "testament" and as "covenant" in the N.T. And

(7) it secures the perpetuity, future conversion, and blessing of a repentant Israel, with whom the New Covenant will yet be ratified (Heb. 10:9, Jer. 31:31-40)." *New Scofield Reference Bible, 1967 by Oxford University Press, Inc.*

The relation of Christ to the eight covenants is as follows:

(1) To the Edenic Covenant, Christ, as the "second man" and the "last Adam" (1 Cor. 15:45-47), takes the place over all things which the first Adam lost (Ccl. 2:10, Heb. 2:7-9).

(2) He is the Seed of the woman of the Adamic Covenant (Gen 3:15; Jn.12:31; Gal. 4:4; 1 Jn. 3:8; Rev. 20:10) and fulfilled its conditions of toil (Mk. 6:3) and obedience (Phil. 2:8; Heb. 5:8).

(3) As the greatest Son of Shem, in Him was fulfilled supremely the promise to Shem in the Noahic Covenant (Gen. 9:16; Col. 2:9).

(4) He is the Seed to whom the promises were made in the Abrahamic Covenant, the Son of Abraham obedient unto death (Gen. 22:18; Gal. 3:16; Phil. 2:8.

(5) He lived sinlessly under the Mosaic Covenant and bore for us its curse (Gal. 3:10-13).

(6) He lived obediently as a Jew in the land under the Palestinian Covenant and will yet perform its gracious promises (Dt. 28:1-30;9).

(7) He is the Seed, Heir, and King under the Davidic Covenant (Mt. 1:1 Lk. 1:31-33). And

(8) His sacrifice is the foundation of the New Covenant (Mt. 26;28; 1 Cor. 11:25). *New*

Scofield Reference Bible.

God will only bless you because of the blood of His covenant and His grace.

We need to establish the basis for receiving God's blessings. The foundation needs to be strong if we are going to build upon it. We need to understand our relationship with God under the Covenant of Grace or the Everlasting Covenant. God will only bless you because of the blood of His Covenant and His grace.

THE NEW COVENANT: "God Himself will establish it through a New Covenant which He will make with Israel when He takes away their sins. This New Covenant is to be made with Israel and Judah and therefore, is not to be confused with the Covenant of Grace which God already has made with the Church. This New Covenant will be unconditional, and thus will not be dependent upon Israel's obedience. See Jeremiah 31:31-32. We do not need to confuse the New Covenant which God is to make with Israel with the Covenant of Grace which God has made with believers in the Lord Jesus Christ." (Donald Barnhouse, Romans volume 4, 11-25-29 page 152.)

"In the OT, *berith* (covenant) identifies three differing types of legal relationships. 1. A two-sided covenant between human parties, both of which voluntarily accept the terms of the agreement (for friendship,) 1 Sam. 18:3-4, marriage, Mal. 2:14; or political alliance, Josh 9:15, Obad 7), God however, never enters in to such a covenant of equality with men. The closest approximation is the *"Covenant of Redemption"* between Jehovah and

Christ (mentioned in certain of the Psalms, 2:7-8; 40: 6-8 under which the Son agrees to undertake man's salvation. But the actual term *berith* is not used." (The Zondervan Pictorial Bible Dictionary, covenant.)

"God the Father and Jesus Christ were the chief originating parties of the *Covenant of Redemption* (Psalm 40:6-8: Heb. 10:5-14 Christ being the Mediator of this covenant, while God and individual men (Heb. 7:9) and God and Israel (Jer. 31-37) were its efficacious partners. The Father and the Son were the chief parties of the Covenant of Grace. God the Father covenanted with Christ to save by grace those who believe in the Son and His substitutionary death. This covenant became the foundation of Romans 4 and Hebrews 11, the two main passages concerning justification by faith in the NT. Individuals in the OT entered into this covenant through their saving faith in and acceptance of the type of Christ in the OT and in the NT by the same faith with acceptance of the antitype, even Jesus Christ Himself." (Wycliffe Bible Encyclopedia, page 386, Covenant.)

"The Covenant of Works, though broken by Adam and though its consequences came upon all mankind, was taken up by Christ, as He was "made of a woman, made under the law, to redeem them that were under the law" (Gal 4:4-5) and kept perfectly by Him for us and in our stead. Further, on the cross He bore the penalty of the broken law for us. We in turn are saved by the Covenant of Grace, which depends upon Christ having ended for us the Covenant of Works; first by fulfilling its demands, and second by bearing its penalties against sin

(Rom. 10:4)." (Wycliffe Bible Encyclopedia, page 391, Covenant.)

"The "New Covenant of Grace" is the gospel or the good news of Jesus Christ. This promise of a New Covenant is for Israel and Judah, or as God calls them in Ezekiel, Israel. But what about the Gentiles? Is the New Covenant of Grace for us? It had better be! There is no other!" (Kay Arthur, Knowing God's Covenant, page 95).

"Miles J. Stanford calls it "The Everlasting Covenant". The Everlasting Covenant of Hebrews 13:20,21 was ratified in eternity past between the Father and the Son, and was fulfilled at the resurrection of Christ. The Everlasting Covenant is neither between God and the Church, nor God and Israel, nor God and the Gentiles. Rather it is between the party of the first part, "the God of peace," and the party of the second part, the "Lord Jesus."

The conditions of this covenant were that if the Great Shepherd would lay down His life for the sheep, the Father would raise Him from among the dead. "And being found in fashion as a man, He humbled Himself, and became obedient unto death, even the death of the Cross." "But God raised Him from the dead..." He was "raised up from the dead by the glory of the Father" (Phil. 2:8; Acts 13:30; Romans 6:4).

The Everlasting Covenant was ratified in eternity past and fulfilled at the resurrection. It is a new covenant in respect to Time (Calvary), and it is new in respect to Kind, I.E. between God the Father and God the Son. It is the fulfillment of Galatians 3:20: "Now a mediator is not a mediator of one, but God is one." We, the Gentiles, become party to the Covenant of Grace because we are in Him and He is in us.

Israel's New Covenant – Israel's New Covenant (Jeremiah 31:31,32; Ezekial 36: 26, 27; 37:14) is between God and kingdom Israel only, and will be inaugurated and fulfilled at the Second Advent. At the current time God is not dealing with nations but with individuals. Israel's New Covenant is based upon the Everlasting Covenant, i.e., the Blood of the Cross

- Galatians 3:14 "...In order that in Christ Jesus the blessing of Abraham might come to the gentiles, so that we might receive the promise of the spirit through faith."

- Hebrews 8: 6-7 "But now He has obtained a more excellent ministry, by as much as He is also the mediator of a *better covenant*, which has been enacted on *better promises*. For if that first covenant had been faultless, there would have been no occasion sought for a second."

Note: The fault was not with the Old Mosaic Covenant, the fault was with us. We couldn't keep it.

The Abrahamic Covenant was a one-way covenant instigated by God towards Abraham. It was only contingent on God's grace.

OLD COVENANT

The Mosaic Covenant (commonly referred to as the Old Covenant) provided a way for God's people to be healed and free from sickness and disease, it was based upon them keeping the law and was contingent upon their obedience. With the law came blessings for obedience and curses for disobedience.

We are under a better covenant because of Christ's sacrifice and His obedience.

- "What the law could not do... God did." Romans 8: 2

This is what we are saved from.

The following are the *bodily* curses for disobedience:

- Deuteronomy 28 (15) "But it shall come about, if you will not obey the Lord your God, to observe to do all His commandments and His statutes which I charge you today, that all these curses shall come upon you and overtake you. (20-22) The Lord will send upon you curses, confusion, and rebuke, in all you undertake to do, until you are destroyed and until you perish quickly, on account of the evil of your deeds, because you have forsaken me. The Lord will make the pestilence cling to you until He has consumed you from the land, where you are entering to possess it. The Lord will smite you with consumption and with fever and with inflammation and with fiery heat and with the sword and with blight and with mildew, and they shall pursue you until you perish. (27-29) The Lord will smite you with the boils of Egypt and with hemorrhoids and with the scab and with the itch, from which you cannot be healed. The Lord will smite you with madness and with blindness and with bewilderment of heart; and you shall grope at noon, as the blind man gropes in darkness, and you shall not prosper in your ways; but you shall only be oppressed and robbed continually, with none to save you. (34-35) And you shall be driven mad by the sight of what you see. The Lord will strike you on the knees and legs with sore boils, from which you cannot be healed, from the sole of your foot to the crown of your head. (45) So all these curses shall come on you and pursue you and overtake you until you are destroyed, because you would not obey the Lord your God by keeping His commandments and His statutes which He commanded you."

Note: There was a woman in our congregation who had an itch that the Dr.'s could not help her with. She was in constant pain and torment due to this itch. At that time the Lord instructed me to tell her that this type of itch was part of the curse as recorded in Deuteronomy 28:27 and had no authority over her because Jesus Christ had taken the curse for us. After prayer the itch went away.

• Deuteronomy 28 continued (58-63) "If you are not careful to observe all the words of this law which are written in this book, to fear this honored and awesome name, The Lord your God, then the Lord will bring extraordinary plagues on you and your descendants, even severe and lasting plagues, and miserable chronic sicknesses. And He will bring back on you all the diseases of Egypt of which you were afraid, and they shall cling to you. *Also every sickness and every plague which, not written in the book of this law,* the Lord will bring on you until you are destroyed. Then you shall be left few in number, whereas you were as the stars of heaven for multitude, because you did not obey the Lord your God. And it shall come about that as the Lord delighted over you to prosper you, and multiply you, so the Lord will delight over you to make you perish and destroy you; and you shall be torn from the land where you are entering to possess it." God is Love! God is Fire!

• After Adam sinned the Lord said. "Cursed is the ground because of you; In toil you will eat of it all the days of your life. Both thorns and thistles it shall grow for you;" Genesis 3:17-19

Note: Did you ever wonder why Jesus wore a crown of thorns on the cross? He took the curse for us.

• "Christ redeemed us from the curse of the law, having become a curse for us. For it is written cursed is everyone who hangs on a tree." Galatians 3:13

Note: If He would not have taken the curse for us, the curse would still be in effect. Because He took the curse, we can expect answers to our prayers for healing as it pertains to those things under the curse in Deuteronomy 28.

SCRIPTURES ON HEALING

The following are passages from the Old Testament on Healing:

A way was provided for healing in the Old Covenant based on obedience. Although many of the Old Covenant promises are not speaking to us directly, by them we can see God's heart and they can only be ours through faith in the finished work of Jesus Christ.

OLD TESTAMENT

• And he said, "If you will give earnest heed to the voice of the Lord your God, and do what is right in His sight, and give ear to His commandments, and keep all His statutes, *I will put none of the diseases on you which I have put on the Egyptians*; for I, the Lord, am your healer." Exodus 15:26

• "But you shall serve the Lord your God, and He will bless your bread and your water; and I will remove sickness from your midst." Exodus 23:25

• "You shall be blessed above all peoples; there shall be no male or female barren among you or among your cattle. And the Lord will remove from you all sickness; and He will not put on you any of the harmful diseases of Egypt which you have known, but He will lay them on all who hate you." Deuteronomy 7: 14-15

• "Now it shall be, if you will diligently obey the Lord your God, being careful to do all His commandments which I command you today, the Lord your God will set you high above all the nations of the earth. And all these blessings shall come upon you and overtake you, if you will obey the Lord your God. Blessed shall you be in the city, and blessed shall you be in the country. Blessed shall be the offspring of your body and the produce of your ground and the offspring of your beasts, the increase of your herd and the young of your flock. Blessed shall be your basket and your kneading bowl. Blessed shall you be when you come in, and blessed shall you be when you go out. The Lord will cause your enemies who rise up against you to be defeated before you; they shall come out against you one way and shall flee before you seven ways. The Lord will command the blessing upon you in your barns and in all that you put your hand to, and He will bless you in the land which the Lord your God gives you." Deuteronomy 28: 1-8

• "The Lord will establish you as a holy people to Himself, as He swore to you, if you will keep the commandments of the Lord your God, and walk in His ways. So all the peoples of the earth shall see that you are called by the name of the

Lord; and they shall be afraid of you. And the Lord will make you abound in prosperity, in the offspring of your body and in the offspring of your beast and in the produce of your ground, in the land which the Lord swore to your fathers to give you. The Lord will open for you His good storehouse, the heavens, to give rain to your land in its season and to bless all the work of your hand; and you shall lend to many nations, but you shall not borrow." Deut. 28: 9-12

•   "I call heaven and earth to witness against you today, that I have set before you life and death, the blessing and the curse. So choose life in order that you may live, you and your descendants, by loving the Lord your God, by obeying His voice, and by holding fast to Him; for this is your life and the length of your days, that you may live in the land which the Lord swore to your fathers, to Abraham, Isaac, and Jacob, to give them." Deuteronomy 30:19-20

•   "Blessed be the Lord, who has given rest to His people Israel, according to all that He promised; not one word has failed of all His good promise, which He promised through Moses His servant." 1 Kings 8:56

•   "The Lord will sustain him upon his sickbed; in his illness, thou dost restore him to health. Psalm 41:3 NASB

•   "O my soul, don't be discouraged. Don't be upset. Expect God to act! For I know that I shall again have plenty of reason to praise him for all that he will do. He is my help! He is my God!" Psalm 42:11 LB

• "For you have made the Lord, my refuge, Even the Most High, your dwelling place. *No evil will befall you, nor will any plague come near your tent.*" Psalm 91:9-10

• "I will fear no evil; for Thou art with me." Psalm 23:4

• "Because he has loved Me, therefore I will deliver him; I will set him securely on high, because he has known My name. He will call upon Me, and I will answer him; I will be with him in trouble; I will rescue him, and honor him. With a long life I will satisfy him, and let him behold My salvation." Psalm 91: 14-16

• "Bless the Lord, O my soul; And all that is within me, bless His holy name. Bless the Lord, O my soul, and forget none of His benefits; Who pardons all your iniquities; *Who heals all your diseases*; Who redeems your life from the pit; Who crowns you with loving kindness and compassion; Who satisfies your years with good things, so that your youth is renewed like the eagle." Psalm 103: 1-5

• "Then they cried out to the Lord in their trouble; He saved them out of their distresses. *He sent His word and healed them*, and delivered them from their destructions. Let them give thanks to the Lord for His lovingkindness, and for His wonders to the sons of men!" Psalm 107:19-21

• "I shall not die, but live, and tell of the works of the Lord." Psalm 118:17

• "Fear the Lord and turn away from evil, *it will be healing to your body,* and refreshment to your bones." Proverbs 3: 7-8

• "My son, give attention to my words; Incline your ear to my sayings. Do not let them depart from your sight; keep them in the midst of your heart. *For they are life to those who find them, and health to all their whole body.* Watch over your heart with all diligence, for from it flow the springs of life. Put away from you a deceitful mouth, and put devious lips far from you." Proverbs 4: 20-24

• "He gives strength to the weary, and to him who lacks might He increases power, though youths grow weary and tired, and vigorous young men stumble badly, yet those who wait for the Lord will gain new strength; They will mount up with wings like eagles, they will run and not get tired, they will walk and not become weary." Isaiah 40: 29-31

• "Do not fear, for I am with you; do not anxiously look about you, for I am your God. I will strengthen you, surely I will help you, surely I will uphold you with My righteous right hand." Isaiah 41: 10

• "Surely our griefs (sickness) He Himself bore, and our sorrows (pain) He carried; yet we ourselves esteemed Him stricken, smitten of God, and afflicted. But He was pierced through for our transgressions, He was crushed for our iniquities; the chastening for our well-being fell upon Him, and by His scourging we are healed." Isaiah 53: 4-5

Note: The Old Testament sacrificial lamb was not beaten up before it was killed. This raises a question. Why was Jesus, the lamb of God, beaten up before He was slain as the sacrifice for our sins? Because He rendered Himself not only as a sin offering, but also as a guilt offering. "But the Lord was pleased to crush Him, putting Him to grief; if He would render Himself as a guilt offering." Isaiah 53:10 "As a result of the anguish of His soul, He will see it and be satisfied;" Isaiah 53:11 The guilt offering is like the sin offering Leviticus 7:7

• "Then your light will break out like the dawn, and your recovery will speedily spring forth; and your righteousness will go before you; the glory of the Lord will be your rear guard." Isaiah 58:8

• "Then the Lord said to me, you have seen well, for I am watching over My word to perform it." Jeremiah 1:12

• "For I will restore you to health and I will heal you of your wounds, declares the Lord, because they have called you an outcast,

saying: It is Zion; no one cares for her."
Jeremiah 30: 17

- "I will bring it health and cure, and I will cure them, and will reveal unto them the abundance of peace and truth." Jeremiah 33:6 KJV

Note: In the Old Testament the blood, not the body, was for forgiveness of sins. The body was burned up. In the New Testament the blood was for forgiveness of sin. The body was not burned up, it was beaten and scourged for us.

Note: Healing has been provided for us while we are on this earth. When we get to heaven we won't need it. We will receive our complete healing when we get to heaven, but for now a way has been provided.

While discussing a man born blind from birth, the disciples asked an interesting question in John 9:2. "Who sinned this man or his parents?" According to the Old Testament way of thinking, they asked the right question. Jesus said, "It was neither that this man sinned nor, his parents; but it was in order that the works of God might be displayed". Jesus then put clay on his eyes he washed and was healed.

THE LAW AND US

The Purpose of the Law

The Law is perfect and just and good. He did not give it that man might be saved by it, but to prove to men that they were sinners.

- "Now we know that whatever the Law says, it speaks to those who are under the Law, that every mouth may be closed, and all the world may become accountable to God; because *by the works of the Law no flesh will be justified in His sight* for through the Law comes the knowledge of sin." Romans 3:19-20

- "So then, the Law is holy, and the commandment is holy and righteous and good.." Romans 7:12

- "Why the Law then? It was added because of transgressions, ...*until* the seed should come to whom the promise had been made." (Christ) Galatians 3:19

Note: The law makes me see that I am a sinner and constantly condemns me. We know that it is right and holy and just, and we know that no matter how hard we try, we just can't be good enough. We just can't live up to its standards under our own power. It does not give me the power to live a godly life. It has no power to keep me from sinning. The Israelites tried it for 1500 years and failed. If it were possible for one person to keep the law, Christ would not have had to die. That one person would have proved that it were possible. If you think the law is hard to keep, try the Sermon on the Mount in Matthew 5.

- "For I say to you, that unless your righteousness surpasses that of the scribes and Pharisees, you shall not enter, the kingdom of heaven." Matthew 5:20

- *"If a law had been given which was able to impart life*, then righteousness would indeed have been based on law." Galatians 3:21

What God Did

- "What the Law could not do, ...God did." Romans 8:3

- "Do not think that I came to abolish the Law or the Prophets; I did not come to abolish, but to fulfill." Matthew 5:20

Romans chapter 7 tells us what God did to free us from the constant condemnation of the *Law of Sin and Death,* so that we could be joined to *the Spirit of Life* in Christ Jesus.

We were married to the Law, and we were bound by the marriage covenant until the death of one of the partners. The Law could not die because it was ordained by God.

- "Therefore, my brethren, you also were made to die to the Law through the body of Christ, that you might be joined to another, to Him who was raised from the dead, that we might bear fruit for God." Romans 7:4

- "But now we have been released from the Law, having died to that by which we were bound, so that we serve in newness of the Spirit and not in oldness of the letter." Romans 7:6

We are now under Grace not under the law. The law can no longer condemn us, we are free from its curse. God freed us from the law so that we might be joined to Christ so that He might live out His righteousness through us.

- "He condemned sin in the flesh in order that the requirement of the law might be fulfilled in us, who do not walk according to the flesh, but according to the Spirit." Romans 8:4

We cannot earn or work for God's blessings. We already have them.

- Galatians 3 "You foolish Galatians, …did you receive the Spirit by the works of the Law, or by hearing with faith? Are you so foolish? Having begun by the Spirit, are you now being perfected by the flesh? Does He then, who provides you with the Spirit and works miracles among you, do it by the works of the Law, or by hearing with faith?

• "Christ redeemed us from the curse of the Law, having become a curse for us, for it is written, "Cursed is everyone who hangs on a tree" - in order that in Christ Jesus the blessing of Abraham might come to the Gentiles, so that we might receive the promise of the Spirit through faith." Galatians 3:14

The Galatians were committing spiritual adultery. Married to one (Christ) trying to have an affair with another (Law).

• "You have been severed from Christ, you who are seeking to be justified by law: you have fallen from grace." Galatians 5:4

• "As you therefore have received Christ Jesus the Lord, so walk in Him." Colossians 2:6

You have received Him by grace through faith, therefore walk in Him by grace through faith.

• Matthew 17: 1-8 "And six days later Jesus took with Him Peter and James and John his brother, and brought them up to a high mountain by themselves. And he was transfigured before them; and His face shone like the sun, and His garments became as white as light. And behold, Moses (Law) and Elijah (Prophets) appeared to them, talking with him. And Peter answered and said to Jesus, "Lord, it is good for us to be here; if You wish, I will make three tabernacles here, one for You, and one for Moses (Law), and one for Elijah (Prophets)." While he was still speaking, behold, a bright cloud overshadowed them; and behold, a voice out of the cloud, saying. "This is My beloved Son, with whom I am well-pleased; hear Him!" And when the disciples heard this, they fell on their faces and were much afraid. And Jesus came to them and touched them and said, "Arise, and do not be afraid." And lifting up their eyes, they saw no one, except Jesus Himself alone."

We do not need three tabernacles, (1) the law, (2) the prophets, (3) and Jesus. We just need Jesus.

• "Do not think I came to abolish the Law or the Prophets; I did not come to abolish, but to fulfill." Matthew 5:17

• "You shall love the Lord your God with all your heart, and with all your soul and with all your mind. This is the first and great commandment. And a second is like unto it. Thou shall love thy neighbor as thyself. *On these two commandments hang all the Law and the Prophets.*" Matthew 22:37-40 KJV

Note: Picture a curtain rod with panels hanging down. On the panels are written all the laws and the prophet's words from God to man. The ends of the curtain rod is held up on one end by the commandment, 'you shall love the Lord your God with all your heart, soul and mind,' and the other end is held up by the commandment 'you shall love your neighbor as yourself'. On these two commandments hang all the law and the prophets.

A Priest brings the message of Man to God, a Prophet brings the message of God to Man. Jesus was Prophet, Priest and King.

- Romans 13: 10 "Love does no wrong to a neighbor; love therefore is the fulfillment of the law."

Note: Be careful of those who say, "If you want to be closer to God you must do this or that." God will bless me not because I can fulfill the requirements of the law, but because Christ has fulfilled the requirements of the law, and I am in Him.

The character of God is shown in the law. We were created to reflect the Glory of God. Why is it wrong to steal? Because God does not steal. We do not lie because God does not lie. We are faithful because God is faithful. Sin is sin because it goes against the character of God.

THE NEW COVENANT

The Old Covenant was between God and His people. The New Covenant of Grace is between God the Father and the Lord Jesus Christ. It is an eternal covenant and cannot be broken.

The reconciliation is between God and Man with Jesus Christ as the mediator of the new covenant fulfilled between God the Father and God the Son, as the Son of Man. (Son means 'of the order of').

A way was provided in the Old Covenant for healing. It was conditional and based on the Law. The New Covenant of Grace is unconditional and demands that blessings are not earned but received by grace through faith in Jesus Christ.

- "Now the God of peace, who brought up from the dead the great Shepherd of the sheep through the blood of the *eternal* covenant, even Jesus our Lord, equip you in every good thing to do His will, working in us that which is pleasing in His sight, through Jesus Christ, to whom be the glory forever and ever. Amen." Hebrews 13:20-21

- "But God, being rich in mercy, because of His great love with which He loved us, even when we were dead in our transgressions, made us alive together with Christ (by grace you have been saved)." Ephesians 2:4-5

• "For by grace you have been saved through faith; and that not of yourselves, it is the gift of God; not as a result of works, that no one should boast." Ephesians 2:8-9

• "Christ redeemed us from the curse of the law, having become a curse for us, for it is written, "Cursed is everyone who hangs on a tree" in order that in Christ Jesus the blessings of Abraham might come to the Gentiles, so that we might receive the *promise* of the Spirit through *faith*." Galatians 3:13-14

• "And if you belong to Christ, then you are Abraham's offspring, heirs according to *promise*." Galatians 3:29

• "Does He then, who provides you with the Spirit and works miracles among you, do it by the works of the Law, or by hearing with faith?" Galatians 3:5

• "And on the basis of faith in His name, it is the name of Jesus which has strengthened this man whom you see and know; and the faith which comes through Him has given him this perfect health in the presence of you all." Acts 3:16

• "He Himself bore our sins in His body on the cross, that we might die to sin and live to righteousness; for by His wounds you were healed." 1 Peter 2:24

In salvation, a person first believes that God can save them. Then he believes that God will save him. And finally, he believes that God has saved him. The same happens in healing, a person believes God can, then God will, and then God has.

Note: In the Old Testament when a man sinned, he would take a sacrifice without spot or blemish, as a substitute for his sins. The Priest would then inspect the lamb or the dove or whatever the sacrifice would be. The Priest would not waste his time inspecting the man. *If the lamb was accepted the man was accepted.* Jesus, the Lamb of God that takes away the sin of the world, is our sacrifice for sin. When we come to the Father with our sacrifice: *The Lamb is accepted, therefore, the man is accepted.*

The only reason God will bless us and hear our prayers is because of the blood of the Lord Jesus Christ. We cannot come to him holding up our own good works or anything we have done.

- "All our righteousness's are as filthy rags". Isaiah 64:6

We shouldn't waste His time or ours by holding up anything but the Lord Jesus Christ when we come to Him in prayer. He is the only reason we can come to the Father in prayer. We did not earn our salvation, we received it by grace through faith. Neither can we earn God's blessings; we can only receive them by grace through faith.

- "As you therefore have received Christ Jesus the Lord, so walk in Him." Colossians 2:6

If we were on a point system then we could win the right to be healed, but we are not on a point system. We cannot earn or work for God's blessings; we already have them. It is our job to accept them and praise Him for His grace.

- "Let us therefore draw near with confidence to the throne of grace, that we may receive mercy and may find grace to help in time of need." Hebrews 4:16

HALLELUJAH!!! *The Lamb was accepted; therefore, I am accepted.*

NEW COVENANT SCRIPTURES

The following are some of the scriptures on healing in the New Covenant of Grace:

SCRIPTURES ON HEALING

- "And behold, a leper came to Him, and bowed down to Him, saying, Lord, if You are willing, You can make me clean. And stretching out His hand, He touched him, saying, I am willing; be cleansed. And immediately his leprosy was cleansed." Matthew 8:2-3

Note: In the Old Covenant when a leper touched a person, the person would become unclean. Jesus, our High Priest, touched a leper and the leper was made whole. Jesus was not contaminated by sin, sin was contaminated by His healing.

- "And when evening had come, they brought to Him many who were demon-possessed; and He cast out the spirits with a word and healed all who were ill in order that what was spoken through Isaiah the prophet might be fulfilled, saying, *He Himself took our infirmities, and carried away our diseases.*" Matthew 8: 16-17, Isaiah 53:4

• "Truly I say to you, whatever you shall bind on earth shall have been bound in heaven; and whatever you loose on earth shall have been loosed in heaven. Again I say to you, that if two of you agree on earth about anything that they may ask, it shall be done for them by My Father who is in heaven." Matthew 18: 18-19

• "And Jesus answered and said to them, truly I say to you, if you have faith, and do not doubt, you shall not only do what was done to the fig tree, but even if you say to this mountain, be taken up and cast into the sea, it shall happen. And everything you ask in prayer, believing, you shall receive." Matthew 21: 21-22, Mark 11:22-24

• "And Jesus said to him, If You can! All things are possible to him who believes." Mark 9:23

• "Looking upon them, Jesus said, with men it is impossible, but not with God; for all things are possible with God." Mark 10:27

• "The thief comes only to steal, and kill, and destroy; I came that they might have life, and might have it abundantly." John 10:10

• "And afterward He appeared to the eleven themselves as they were reclining at table; and He reproached them for their unbelief and hardness of heart, because they had not believed those who had seen Him after He had risen. And He said to them, Go into all the world and preach the gospel to all creation. He who has believed and has been baptized shall be saved; but he who has disbelieved shall be condemned. And these signs will accompany those who have believed: in My name they will cast out demons, they will speak with new tongues; they will pick up serpents, and if they drink any deadly poison, it shall not hurt them; they will lay hands on the sick, and they will recover." Mark 16:14-18

Note: Chemotherapy is a deadly poison. It is designed to kill cancer. Pray that it would do the job it is intended to do. Pray every time you have a chemotherapy treatment.

• "Lord...grant that Thy bond-servants may speak Thy word with all confidence, while Thou doest extend Thy hand to heal, and signs and wonders take place through the name of Thy holy servant Jesus." Acts 4:29-30

• "And on the basis of faith in His name, it is the Name of Jesus which has strengthened this man whom you see and know; and the faith which comes through Him has given him this perfect health in the presence of you all." Acts 3:16

• "But if the Spirit of Him who raised Jesus from the dead dwells in you, He who raised Christ Jesus from the dead will also give life to your mortal bodies through His Spirit who indwells you." Romans 8:11

• "Faith comes from hearing, and hearing by the word of Christ." Romans 10:17

• "For he who eats and drinks, eats and drinks judgment to himself, if he does not judge the body rightly. For this reason many among you are weak and sick, and a number sleep." 1 Corinthians 11:29-30

• "For to one is given by the Spirit the word of wisdom; to another the word of knowledge by the same Spirit; To another faith by the same Spirit: to another the gifts of healing by the same Spirit." 1 Corinthians 12: 8-9

• "Does He then, who provides you with the Spirit and works miracles among you, do it by the works of the law, or by hearing with faith?" Galatians 3:5

• "He raised Him from the dead, and seated Him at His right hand in the heavenly places, far above all rule and authority and power and dominion, and every name that is named, *not only in this age,* but also in the one to come." Ephesians 1:20-21

• "Is anyone among you sick? Let him call for the elders of the church, and let them pray over him, anointing him with oil in the name of the Lord: and the prayer offered in faith will restore the one who is sick and the Lord will raise him up, and if he has committed sins, they will be forgiven him." James 5:14-15 KJV

•	"Admit your faults to one another and pray for each other so that you may be healed. The earnest prayer of a righteous man has great power and wonderful results. James 5:16 LB

•	"Now may the God of peace himself sanctify you entirely: and may your spirit, soul and body be preserved complete, without blame at the coming of our Lord Jesus Christ." 1 Thessalonians 5:23

•	"He personally carried the load of our sins in his own body when He died on the cross, so that we can be finished with sin and live a good life from now on, for His wounds have healed ours!" 1 Peter 2:24 LB

I don't want my children struggling to obtain My blessings.

KNOWING GOD'S WILL

Jesus came to do the will of the Father.
The majority of Jesus' recorded ministry on earth was healing the sick in spirit, soul or body. Would you say it was God's will for His people to be made whole?

- "Jesus answered and was saying to them, "Truly, truly, I say to you, the Son can do nothing of Himself, unless it is something He sees the Father doing; for whatever the Father does, these things the Son also does in like manner." John 5:19

- "For I did not speak on My own initiative, but the Father Himself who sent Me has given Me commandment, what to say, and what to speak." John 12:49

- "I can do nothing on My own initiative. As I hear, I judge; and My judgment is just, because I do not seek My own will, but the will of Him who sent Me." John 5:30

- "the works which the Father has given Me to accomplish, the very works that I do, bear witness of Me, that the Father has sent Me." John 5:36

- "He who has seen Me has seen the Father." John 14:9

- "Do you not believe that I am in the Father, and the Father is in Me? The words that I say to you I do not speak on My own initiative, but the Father abiding in Me does His works." John 14:10

- "You know of Jesus of Nazareth, how God anointed Him with the Holy Sprit and with power, and how He went about doing *good*, and healing all who were oppressed by the devil; for God was with Him." Acts 10:38

- "And Jesus was going about in all Galilee, teaching in their synagogues, and proclaiming the gospel of the kingdom, and *healing* every kind of disease and every kind of sickness among the people. And the news about Him went out into all Syria; and they brought to Him all who were ill, taken with various *diseases* and *pains*, demoniacs, epileptics, paralytics; and He healed them." Matthew 4:23-24

Note: I have a friend, named Mark, who was at a hospital visiting a woman who was in hospice and in intense pain. He asked the Lord if he could pray for her healing and the Lord said, "no". He than asked may I pray for relief from the pain and the Lord said, "yes". My friend then laid his hands on the woman and prayed for the pain and immediately a calm came over her face and everybody in the room saw how her countenance had changed. Mark thought that after seeing such a remarkable change in her that the Lord had healed her after all. A week later he went back to the hospital and the nurse said she had passed away, but she had never before seen a person with that disease die with no pain and at total peace. He not only heals diseases but also pains. Praise God for His grace!

- "And when evening had come, they brought to Him many who were demon-possessed; and He cast out the spirits with a word, and healed all who were ill in order that what was spoken through Isaiah the prophet might be fulfilled, saying, HE HIMSELF TOOK OUR INFIRMITIES, AND CARRIED AWAY OUR DISEASES." Matthew 8:16 -17

- "And Jesus was going about all the cities and the villages, teaching in their synagogues, and proclaiming the gospel of the kingdom, and healing every kind of disease and every kind of sickness." Matthew 9:35

- "But the Pharisees went out, and counseled together against Him, as to how they might destroy Him. But Jesus, aware of this, withdrew from there. And many followed Him, and He *healed them all*." Matthew 12:14-15

- "And when He came out, He saw a great multitude, and felt compassion for them, and healed their sick." Matthew 14:14

- "And while the sun was setting, all who had any sick with various diseases brought them to Him; and laying His hands on every one of them, He was healing them." Luke 4:40

•   "And these signs will accompany those who have believed: in My name they will cast out demons, they will speak with new tongues; they will pick up serpents, and if they drink any deadly poison, it shall not hurt them; they will lay hands on the sick, and they will recover." Mark 16:17-18

•   "Jesus therefore said to them again, Peace be with you; as the Father has sent Me, I also send you." John 20:21

•   "As Thou didst send Me into the world, I also have sent them into the world." John 17:18

•   "And having summoned His twelve disciples, He gave them authority over unclean spirits, to cast them out, and to heal every kind of disease and every kind of sickness." Matthew 10:1

Note: It was important for Jesus to give the disciples the authority to do these things at that time because the Holy Spirit had not yet been poured out. They needed a time of learning with Jesus to know how to properly use what was given them.

•   "I do not ask in behalf of these alone, but for those also who believe in Me through their word; that they may all be one; even as Thou, Father, are in Me, and I in Thee, that they also may be in Us; that the world may believe that Thou didst send Me. And the glory which Thou hast given Me I have given to them; that they may be one, just as We are one: I in them, and Thou in Me, that they may be perfected in unity, that the world may know that Thou didst send Me, and didst love them, even as Thou didst love Me." John 17: 20-23

• *God's will is not always done upon the earth. We have an enemy who will do everything he can to make sure God's will is not done. We must pray for those who are sick so that God's will, will be done.*

• "Put on the full armor of God, that you may be able to stand firm against the schemes of the devil. For our struggle is not against flesh and blood, but against the rulers, against the powers, against the world forces of this darkness, against the spiritual forces of wickedness in the heavenly places." Ephesians 6:11-12

He would not have given us the armor if He didn't think we needed it

• "You are my war club, my weapon of war". Jeremiah 51:20.

In the days of yore, the "Knights of The Round Table" had their own distinct armor. If you saw a man coming on a horse who wore Sir Lancelot's armor, you would say, "Look here comes Sir Lancelot." We are told to put on the armor of God so that we can stand against the schemes of the devil. When the enemy sees us coming in God's armor, who does he think is coming after him?

• "But if the Spirit of Him who raised Jesus from the dead dwells in you, He who raised

Christ Jesus from the dead will also give life to your *mortal* bodies through His Spirit who indwells you." Romans 8:11

Note: We have *mortal* (subject to death) bodies as we walk this earth. One day we will have *immortal* bodies (not subject to death).

IF OR BECAUSE
(Law or Grace)

The Old Covenant is based on the law and says: If you do this or that God will bless you. The New Covenant is based on the grace of God and the shed blood of Jesus Christ. The only reason God will bless you today is because of His Grace and the price having been paid by the shed blood of Jesus Christ.

Many Christians fail to receive the blessings of God because they try to base receiving them on the basis of their good works.

- "Without faith it is impossible to please Him." Hebrews 11:6

- "And all our righteous deeds are like a filthy garment;" Isaiah 64:6

Note: *Let's take the example of tithing for instance.*

- "Bring the whole tithe into the storehouse, so that there may be food in My house, and test Me now in this," says the Lord of Hosts, if I will not open for you the windows of heaven, and pour out for you a blessing until there is no more need." Malachi 3:10

The Lord says, "If you tithe, I will bless you." Why are we blessed? We are blessed because of the Grace of God and the shed blood of Jesus Christ. If, not because, I tithe God will bless me. God's blessings cannot be earned. If blessings could be earned, then it would not be of grace. In the same way healing has to be based on the Grace of God and because of the shed blood of Jesus Christ.

- "Christ redeemed us from the curse of the Law, having become a curse for us- for it is written, "Cursed is everyone who hangs on a tree"- in order that in Christ Jesus the blessings of Abraham might come to the Gentiles..." Galatians 3:13-14

Note: You will hear people say, "God should heal that person, they've been so good all their lives; they sang in the choir, taught Sunday school, tithed, and did all the right things." God will not heal you because of what you've done, but because of what He's done, and His great love for us.

The Christian Life is not a matter of us walking on the earth struggling to do God's will. It is us allowing Christ to walk on the earth doing His will through us.

DOCTORS AND MEDICINE

God can and does heal through doctors and medicine. God can work much better through a Christian doctor that is led by the Holy Spirit than through an unbeliever. The Christian doctor is more open to God's leading and has God's wisdom and knowledge at his disposal.

Note: If a person believes that it is not God's will to heal today then he has no right to go to a doctor because he would be actively going against his belief.

- "…Asa became diseased in his feet. His disease was severe, yet even in his disease he did not seek the Lord but the physicians. So Asa slept with his fathers…" 2 Chronicles 16:12-13

The Lord was displeased not that Asa sought the physicians, but that he sought the physicians *instead* of the Lord.

Somehow Christians feel that they are more spiritual if they do not go to a doctor but simply trust the Lord to heal. We are to pray about the Lord's direction in our lives for everything, including going to the doctor when we are ill. If He leads you to go to a doctor then, by all means, go. Maybe He would like to heal you through the doctor.

- Paul said to Timothy: "No longer drink water exclusively, but use a little wine for the sake of your stomach and your frequent ailments." 1 Timothy 5:23

Note: Wine was used for medicinal purposes in those days the same as people using medicine today. The key point is not whether you do or don't use them it is how you use them. It is of first importance to seek the Lord's will and if He leads you to use medicine then pray that the Lord will work through the medicine and allow it to work the way He intends for it to work. Medicine does not heal, it simply gives the body an opportunity to heal; you still need to be bathed in prayer and faith in God's word.

Almost all hospitals were started by Christians or Christian organizations, because they knew it was God's will to heal.

If you pray about an illness and God instructs you to go to a doctor. Then go and listen to the doctor and if he gives you medication to take. Take it at the prescribed time and for the prescribed time. I would suggest, however, that you pray over every dosage and ask the Lord to allow that medication to do its job in your body. If you disobey the doctor you may be disobeying God because He told you to go to the doctor.

Note: In November of 2006, during our Wednesday Night Prayer meeting. I handed out the prayer requests and Pat said that she had broken her foot on the way to prayer meeting and asked if one of us could take her to the hospital. I asked to look at her foot and there was a bone poking up on the top of her foot. It had not gone through the skin. I asked her if we could pray for her before we took her to the hospital. As she was sitting in the chair, I was standing behind her, with my hands on her shoulders. Marilyn knelt down and was holding her foot in her hand. As I was praying, Marilyn said, "The bones are moving in my hand." She asked Pat "can you feel the bones moving?" she said, "Yes I can". Praise God! The bones were put back into place. At the hospital they took x-rays and the Dr. said it was broken, but all the bones are in place and there is no need for an operation.

A woman asked for prayer at our Wednesday morning prayer meeting. She had dislocated her shoulder and her arm was in a sling. When she came forward for prayer, I put my hand gently on her shoulder. As I prayed for her, I could feel the bones moving in her shoulder. The Lord was putting it back in place. It wasn't long and she took off the sling and gave it to her husband. By the time she left the meeting she was completely healed. Most people in the meeting did not know what had occurred because we didn't make a big deal out of it. The Lord just did His thing and healed her.

Most people are not against healing, they are against God doing it.

COMMUNION

There are two ordinances in the church – Water Baptism and Communion. Water Baptism is an ordinance of the church that is more than just washing with water. Water Baptism is an outward expression of an inward blessing.

Communion is an ordinance of the church and it too is more than just taking bread and wine as a nice tradition. It too is an outward expression of an inward blessing.

I will agree there are counterfeit teachings about communion however, we cannot be so afraid of the counterfeit that we refuse to teach the truth.

When you stand before a court of law, the judge can judge you guilty or innocent of the charges against you. When taking communion you may judge your body in a negative way or a positive way. We are encouraged to judge our body rightly.

Why are many among you weak and sick, and a number sleep?

•   "…He took bread, and when He had given thanks, He broke it, and said, "This is My body, which is for you; do this in *remembrance* of Me." In the same way He took the cup also, after supper, saying, "This cup is the new covenant in

My blood; do this, as often as you drink it, in *remembrance* of Me." 1 Corinthians 11: 24-25

• "But let a man examine himself, and so let him eat of the bread and drink of the cup. For he who eats and drinks, eats and drinks judgment to himself, if he does not judge the *body* rightly. For this reason many among you are weak and sick, and a number sleep. But if we judged ourselves rightly, we should not be judged." 1 Corinthians 11: 28-31

Note: If we judged the body rightly, we would say: "I remember that: My body is a temple of the Holy Spirit; Jesus Christ lives in my body. The body of Jesus is not sick or diseased, but it is whole and full of life. The mind of Christ, is not confused or disturbed, but it is at peace and calm, trusting in Jesus. When I take Christ's body into my body, darkness has to flee, and the light will overcome darkness. Where light enters, darkness has to flee. The body of Christ that I have in my body is not sick or diseased, but is well and whole and in a right standing with the Father because of the sacrifice of His Son. I forgive all who have ever wronged me, and I hold no animosity or grudge toward anyone because the love of God has been poured into my heart through the Holy Spirit who was given to me, according to Romans 5:5.

Note: His body was broken so mine could be made whole.

• "He Himself bore our sins in His body on the cross that we might die to sin and live to righteousness; for by His wounds you were healed." 1 Peter 2:24

- "For the death that He died, He died to sin, once for all; but the life that He lives, He lives to God, even so consider yourselves to be dead to sin, but alive to God in Christ Jesus." Romans 6: 10-11.

Note: He died not only for our sin, represented by the Blood but He also died to our sin represented by the Body.

"The Blood can wash away my sins, but it cannot wash away my 'old man'. It needs the cross to crucify me...the sinner...Our sins are dealt with by the Blood, but we ourselves are dealt with by the Cross. The Blood procures our pardon...the Cross procures our deliverance from what we are". (Watchman Nee).

Alcoholism, drugs, addictions, pornography, greed, bad temper, stealing, lying, gossip, depression. All these things are subject to the authority of Christ and have to leave my body because the Spirit of Christ has taken up residence there.

Anything that is not of God is to be subject to the authority of Christ and has to flee my body when the body of Christ comes in. His name is above all names and at the Name of Jesus, the name of cancer, diabetes, high blood pressure, stroke, heart disease and any other disease that has a name has to bow to the Name of Jesus and His authority.

This is true whether we take communion or not, however communion gives a tangible opportunity to remember. It gives a point of *remembrance* as an anchor so that we can judge the body rightly.

We do not battle the flesh with the flesh. We battle the flesh by standing on the finished work of Jesus Christ.

We were redeemed by His blood so that we can share His body.

- "Is not the cup of blessing which we bless a sharing in the blood of Christ. Is not the bread which we break a sharing in the body of Christ?" 1 Corinthians 10:16

- "Therefore whoever eats the bread or drinks the cup of the Lord in an *unworthy* manner, shall be guilty of the body and the blood of the Lord." 1 Corinthians 11:27

Many religions stress how unworthy we are. We should stress how worthy we are, not because of our righteous deeds but because of the sacrifice of the Son. We should take communion in a worthy manner.

Sickness and Disease are never punishment for our sin, Christ took our punishment for us. It however could be a natural consequence of sin.

- "Thou dost prepare a table before me in the presence of my enemies." Psalm 23:5

Dead To Sin

As a Christian if I told you that Jesus Christ died *for* your sin you would believe it and would have no problem telling me the story of salvation. You would probably tell me how He died for me and paid the penalty of my sin and how He was the sacrifice for my sin. But do you realize that He also died *to* sin.

- "For the death He died, He died to sin, once for all: but the life that He lives, He lives to God." Romans 6:10

He died to sin one time for everyone. The fact that He died to sin was as our substitute. This gives us the victory over the power of sin in our lives. It's important to realize that we were incapable of that death because we were already dead in trespasses and sin.

He died to sin in our place. We are in Christ and Christ is in us. His death became effective on the cross. It became effective in my behavior when I counted it as true in my daily walk. Many times Paul used the word *reckon* which means to *count as true*.

- "How shall we who died to sin still live in it?" Romans 6:2

- "Knowing this that our old self was crucified with Him, that our body of sin might be done away with, that we should no longer be slaves to sin;" Romans 6:6

- "Even so consider yourselves to be dead to sin, but alive to God in Christ Jesus." Romans 6:11

- "For you have died and your life is hidden with Christ in God." Colossians 3:3

- "I have been crucified with Christ; and it is no longer I who live, but Christ lives in me; and the life I now live in the flesh I live by faith in the Son of God, who loved me, and delivered himself up for me." Galatians 2:20

"God looks upon us as having died with Christ, and this fact makes possible the triumph of the Christian life." (Barnhouse)

This victory over sin in the life of a Christian is not attained by some 12-step program. It is appropriated through the death, burial and resurrection of Jesus Christ. The death of Christ occurred over 2,000 years ago it became effective in my behavior when I reckoned it so in my daily behavior.

Sin has not died, it is still very active and all around us. We are to reckon ourselves to be dead to sin.

"The old Adamic nature cannot be cured, trained, polished, or cleaned. It can only be crucified with Christ." (Barnhouse)

We need the victory over the sin in our lives now. We won't need it when we die and go to heaven. There won't be any sin. We can have the victory over sins power by standing on the finished work of Christ. When we go to heaven we will be delivered from sins presence.

You will discover that after realizing that you are dead to sin you have only come half way. The next step is to reckon on the fact that you are alive unto God through the resurrection of Christ.

Do not battle the flesh with the flesh!

ADOPTION

- "For ye have not received the spirit of bondage again to fear; but ye have received the Spirit of adoption, whereby we cry, Abba, Father." Romans 8:15

As you know, according to John 3:3, the only way to become a child of God is to be born into the family. In Romans 8:15 Paul uses the word adoption which is different than our view of adoption.

There was a Roman and Greek ceremony that Paul was referring to. This ceremony was portrayed in the movie *The Robe*. When a child had reached a certain age set forth by the father, he was taken to the temple where all the rights of the father were bestowed. With speeches and much pomp, clean shaven for the first time, he was given a family robe, a signet ring and sandals for his feet. From that time on he was never treated as a child but as a son with all the rights and privileges of the father.

Paul further explains this custom in Galatians Chapter 4:1-7. "Now I say, as long as the heir is a child, he does not differ at all from a slave although he is owner of everything, but he is under guardians and managers until the date set by the father. So also we, while we were children, were held in bondage under the elemental things of the world. But when the fullness of the time came, God sent forth His Son, born of a woman, born under the Law, in order that He might redeem those who were under the law, that we might receive the adoption as sons. And because you are sons, God has sent forth the Spirit of His Son into our hearts, crying, "Abba! Father!" Therefore you are no longer a slave, but a son; and if a son, then an heir through God."

Notice in the story of the prodigal son as recorded in Luke 15:11-32. When the son returned in verse 22, the father said to his slaves, "Quickly bring out the best robe and put it on him, and put a ring on his hand and sandals on his feet," All the rights and privileges as a son were instantly bestowed on him again.

There are those who refuse to come to the Lord for healing due to some past sin, They feel that they must suffer the consequences of their actions and therefore the Lord will not heal them. Tell me how much suffering is enough? You may have been carrying that burden for many years. It has kept you from walking in all the rights and privileges that are yours in Christ Jesus. It's as though the locust has come in and destroyed your crops.

- "Then I will make up to you for the years that the swarming locust has eaten." Joel 2:25

- "If we confess our sins, He is faithful and righteousness to forgive us our sins and to cleanse us from all unrighteousness." 1 John 1:9

- "All scripture is inspired by God and profitable for teaching, for reproof, for correction, for training in righteousness; that the man of God may be adequate, equipped for every good work." 2 Timothy 3:16-17

Scripture is used for teaching, reproof and correction, not sickness and disease. You may learn something from it but that is not its purpose.

- "The thief comes only to steal, and kill, and destroy; I came that they might have life, and might have it abundantly." John 10:10

We were redeemed by His death so that we can share His life.

SAYING

We are to call things that are not as though they are. We are not to call things that are as though they are not.

- "…in the sight of Him whom he believed, even God, who gives life to the dead and calls into being that which does not exist." Romans 4:17

- "…God has chosen, the things that are not, that He might nullify the things that are." 1 Corinthians 1:28

- "…we look not at the things which are seen, but at the things which are not seen; for the things which are seen are temporal, but the things which are not seen are eternal." 2 Corinthians 4:18

- "Now faith is the assurance of things hoped for, the conviction of things not seen." Hebrews 11:1

Christian Science calls things that are as though they are not, a form of denial. As Christians we admit the problem and call upon the Lord's healing and wholeness. We are to call things that are not as though they are.

• "For verily I say unto you, that whosoever shall *say* unto this mountain, Be thou removed, and be thou cast into the sea; and shall not doubt in his *heart*, but shall believe that those things which he *saith* shall come to pass; he shall have whatsoever he *saith*." Mark 11:23

Note: Three times in the above passage the Lord stresses the importance of what we say. You should also notice the importance of not doubting in your heart, it does not say, do not doubt in your mind. For out of the heart proceed the issues of life. We cannot reduce faith to nothing more than a mental exercise.

• "For with the heart man believes, resulting in righteousness, and with the mouth he confesses, resulting in salvation." Romans 10:10

• "For we all stumble in many ways. If any one does not stumble in what he says, he is a perfect man, able to bridle the whole *body* as well." James 3:2

• "If any one thinks himself to be religious; and yet does not bridle his tongue but deceives his own heart, this man's religion is worthless." James 1:26

• "Let no unwholesome word proceed from your mouth, but only such a word as is good for edification according to the need of the moment, that it may give grace to those who hear, and do not grieve the Holy Spirit of God, by whom you were sealed for the day of redemption. Let all bitterness and wrath and anger and clamor and slander be put away from you, along with all malice. And be kind to one another, tender-hearted, forgiving each other, just as God in Christ also has forgiven you." Ephesians 4:29-32

• "Therefore strengthen the hands that are weak and the knees that are feeble, and make straight paths for your feet, so that the limb which is lame may not be put out of joint, but rather be healed." Hebrews 12 12-13

• "And so, as those who have been chosen of God, holy and beloved, put on a heart of compassion, kindness, humility, gentleness and patience; bearing with one another, and forgiving each other, whoever has a complaint against any one; just as the Lord forgave you, so also should you." Colossians 3:12-13

Keep your saying consistent with your praying. You can mess up a good prayer with an unbelieving confession.

Do you speak to your problems or about them?

• "But having the same spirit of faith, according to what is written, I BELIEVED, THEREFORE I SPOKE, we also believe, therefore also we speak;" 2 Corinthians 4:13

- "This you know, my beloved brethren. But let every one be quick to hear, *slow to speak* and slow to anger;" James 1:19

Note: The word "doubt" comes from the root word "double".

- "But if any of you lacks wisdom, let him ask of God, who gives to all men generously and without reproach, and it will be given to him. But let him ask in faith without any doubting, for the one who doubts is like the surf of the sea driven and tossed by the wind. For let not that man expect that he will receive anything from the Lord, being a double-minded man, unstable in all his ways." James 1:5-8

Note: God will give to all men generously "without reproach". He will not say, "you've done things so stupidly you deserve what you get."

To Say, is An Act of faith.

- "Behold, the ships also, though they are so great and are driven by strong winds, are still directed by a very small rudder, wherever the inclination of the pilot desires. So also the *tongue* is a fire, the very world of iniquity; the *tongue* is set among our members as that which defiles the entire *body*, and sets on fire *the course of our life*, and is set on fire by hell." James 3: 4-5

A large ship is turned by a small rudder, as soon as the rudder is moved the ship starts to turn, however, it may take a long time to turn around a large ship. The same is true with what we say, it may take a long time to see results, but things are turning.

One way of being a *doer* of the word is being a *sayer* of the word.

- "Pleasant words are a honeycomb, sweet to the soul and *healing* to the bones." Proverbs 16:24

- "Death and life are in the power of the *tongue*, And those who love it will eat its fruit." Proverbs 18:21

- "I will guard my ways, that I may not sin with my tongue; I will guard my mouth as with a muzzle, while the wicked are in my presence." Psalm 39:1

- "The tongue of the wise brings healing." Proverbs 12:18

- "You will also *decree* a thing, and it will be established for you; And light will shine on your ways." Job 22:28

We are to speak words of healing, assurance, restoration, victory, power and wisdom, and as we do, we will become stronger and bolder and we will increase in revelation and the knowledge of God.

Note: *I try not to take ownership of a disease with my words. It is not my cancer or diabetes or heart problem. It is cancer or diabetes or a heart problem that is in my body and I need a Savior.*

Speaking words of faith will help your faith.

Be a person of integrity – can other people trust what you say. If they cannot believe what you say, how will they believe you when you tell them about the things of God?

JESUS WAS GLORIFIED

The Holy Spirit could not be poured out in Acts chapter 2 until Jesus was glorified. According to John 7: 38-39 Jesus said, "He who believes in me, as the scriptures said, from his innermost being shall flow rivers of living water. But this He spoke of the Spirit, whom those who believed in Him were to receive; for the Spirit was not yet given, because Jesus was not yet glorified."

While Jesus was on the earth in John 17: 4-5 He prayed, "I glorified Thee on the earth, having accomplished the work which Thou hast given me to do. And now, glorify Thou Me together with Thyself, Father, with the glory which I ever had with Thee before the world was."

Jesus longed to be clothed with the glory He had throughout eternity. Something needed to happen before the Holy Spirit could be poured out. Did His death release the outpouring of the Holy Spirit? No! Did His resurrection release the outpouring of the Holy Spirit? No! His death and resurrection qualified Him, as the Son of Man, to be glorified.

Jesus the Lamb of God was our sacrifice to the Father. Proof that the sacrifice was complete was God raised Him from the dead. He then presented Himself to the Father to be glorified with the glory that He had from the foundation of the world.

- "And gathering them together, He commanded them not to leave Jerusalem, but to wait for what the Father had promised. 'Which,' He said, 'you heard of from Me; for John baptized with water, but you shall be baptized with the Holy Spirit, not many days from now'." Acts 1:4-5

The disciples were ordered to wait until they received what the Father had promised. The Holy Spirit could not be given until Jesus was glorified. They waited because Jesus told them to wait. In fact, He told them "don't do anything until you receive what the Father had promised." They didn't know what they were waiting for or what it would look like when they saw it. But still they waited. Maybe they missed it, they thought. Weeks became a month, and it wasn't until 50 days had passed that the promise was given. Instantly they knew that Jesus Was Glorified! The outpouring of the Holy Spirit was proof that *Jesus was glorified.*

- "And a certain man who had been lame from his mother's womb was being carried along, whom they used to set down every day at the gate of the temple which is called Beautiful, in order to beg alms of those entering the temple. And when he saw Peter and John about to go into the temple, he began asking to receive alms. And Peter, along with John, fixed his gaze upon him and said, "Look at us!" And he began to give them his attention, expecting to receive something from them. But Peter said, "I do not possess silver and gold, but what I do have I give to you; In the name of Jesus Christ the Nazarene-walk!" And seizing him by the right hand, he raised him up; and immediately his feet and his ankles were strengthened." Acts 3:2-8

• "Men of Israel, why do you marvel at this, or why do you gaze at us, as if by our own power or piety we had made him walk? The God of Abraham, Isaac, and Jacob, the God of our Fathers, has glorified His Servant Jesus," Acts 3:12-13

This man was not healed so that Jesus could be glorified in the healing, although that may be true. Jesus was glorified in the healing. Peter is stating this man was healed *because* Jesus was glorified. Because Jesus was glorified by the Father with the glory He had from the foundation of the world, the Holy Spirit was poured out and this man was healed. You want to know how was this man healed? I'll tell you how this man was healed, because Jesus was *Glorified*. His atoning sacrifice was accepted by the Father. His resurrection was accepted by the Father. His work was finished and He was glorified by the Father. The God of our Fathers, has glorified His Servant Jesus. Because He was glorified, the manifestation of the presence of God, the Holy Spirit, was released and this man was healed. Now Peter could say, in power, by His wounds you were healed. 1 Peter 2:24

• "Therefore having been exalted to the right hand of God, and having received from the Father the promise of the Holy Spirit, He has poured forth this which you both see and hear." Acts 2:33

His death and resurrection have qualified us to be glorified in Him. His glorification has become our glorification. What is the pre-requisite for you to receive the baptism (identification) of the Holy Spirit? Jesus was glorified! We can stand in the presence of God for healing because Jesus was glorified, and we are glorified in Him. "Christ in you the hope of glory." Colossians 1:27.

FAITH

There are three types of faith mentioned in the Bible— (1) Saving Faith, (2) The Fruit of the Spirit type of faith, and (3) The Gift of the Spirit, Faith. Everybody has normal faith like sitting on a chair and believing it will hold you, this is not the type of faith the Bible talks about.

Real faith is not mental assent; it is a spiritual gift - given by the Spirit of God. It has its origin in God not in your mind. Faith that is based upon mental assent is called metaphysical.

Real faith is not apathy. (Oh well, all things work together for good.) That is fatalism (The Moslems say, if a person is hit by a car, Ala wills it.) Faith is an active gift of God, not a passive mental exercise.

Real faith is spiritual not intellectual. Faith must get past your head and into your heart. To believe means to trust in and totally rely on. It is possible to give mental assent to something without having it in your heart. How many times did you have to hear the gospel before you got it in your heart and trusted in and totally relied on the finished work of Christ for your salvation.

- "So faith comes from hearing, and hearing by the word of Christ." Romans 10:17

- "For with the *heart* man believes, resulting in righteousness, and with the mouth he confesses, resulting in salvation." Romans 10:10

Faith is mentioned 300 times in the New Testament only twice in the Old Testament. Deuteronomy 32:20 (no faith) Habakkuk 2:4 (prophecy of faith)

- "Fixing our eyes on Jesus, the author and perfecter of faith." Hebrews 12:2

(1) Saving Faith is a gift of God to the lost so they can receive the gift of salvation.

- "For by grace you have been saved through faith; and that not of yourselves, it is the gift of God." Ephesians 2:8

- "That the God of our Lord Jesus Christ, the Father of glory, may give you a spirit of wisdom and of revelation in the knowledge of Him." Ephesians 1:17

We don't need more information, we need more revelation.

- "I pray that the eyes of your *heart may be enlightened*, so that you may know what is the hope of His calling, what are the riches of the glory of His inheritance in the saints, and what is the surpassing greatness of His power toward us who believe." Ephesians 1:18

(2) The Fruit of Faith is given to every born-again believer.

• "...as God has allotted to each a measure of faith." Romans 12:3

• "But the fruit of the Spirit is love, joy, peace, long-suffering, gentleness, goodness, *faith*, meekness, temperance: against such there is no law." Galatians 5:22

The fruit of faith can grow as we get into God's word, it can be nourished and increased the more we read and believe the word.

• "Faith comes from hearing, and hearing by the word of Christ." Romans 10:17

Note: *You may ask. I know that the Lord has given me faith but how can I get my faith to work?*

• "...Faith which worketh by love." Galatians 5:6 KJV

• "Faith activated and energized and expressed and working through love." Galatians 5:6 Amplified

Look at the love of God. If your faith is not working, it is a lack of understanding the love of God, not a lack of faith.
God's word puts your eyes on God, not on your faith. Ask not how big is my faith, instead how big is my God.

• "Now for this very reason, applying all diligence, in your faith supply moral excellence, and in your moral excellence, knowledge; and in your knowledge, self-control, and in your self-control, perseverance, and in your perseverance, godliness, and in your godliness, brotherly kindness, and in your brotherly kindness, Christian love. For if these qualities are yours and are increasing, they render you neither useless nor unfruitful in the true knowledge of our Lord Jesus Christ." 2 Peter 1:5-8

THE GIFT OF FAITH

(3) **The Gift of Faith is a sudden surge of Faith, usually in a crisis, to confidently believe in your heart, without a doubt, that as we act or speak in Jesus' Name, it shall come to pass.**

Acts chapter 3 shows this kind of faith in action. Peter and John went to the Temple every day. The beggar was laid at the gate of the Temple every day. He looked at Peter and John expecting to receive something, probably because he had received something in the past. This particular day the gift of faith to perform healing came upon Peter and John and they did not pray about it but said; "In the name of Jesus Christ of Nazareth. Rise up and walk." This sudden surge of faith could not be conjured up or mentally explained, it was a gift of God for that particular situation.

Note: The beggar did not have to go through physical therapy to learn how to walk.

One time I was walking past a television store and the Lord told me to go in and talk to the owner. I obeyed and he accepted Christ, but what I didn't know was his eighty-year-old father was in the back room and was listening to our conversation; he also came to the Lord.

This also happened to me in church one day. A couple was sitting in the pew ahead of us and the Lord said to lay your hands on her and pray for her back. I did and she was instantly healed of long-standing back problems. I had no idea she had back problems and knew nothing about her health situation before I prayed, I simply acted in faith.

> • "Now concerning spiritual gifts, brethren, I do not want you to be unaware... But to each one is given the manifestation of the Spirit for the common good.... For to one is given the word of wisdom through the Spirit, and to another the word of knowledge according to the same Spirit: to another faith by the same Spirit, and to another gifts of healing by the one Spirit... But one and the same Spirit works all these things, distributing to each one individually as He wills." 1 Corinthians 12:1-11

When praying for a person's healing, look for the Gift of Faith. If the Gift of Faith is not imparted, then go with the Fruit of Faith. The Gift of Faith may be imparted as you use the Fruit of Faith.

Note: One day I was called to a person's home to pray for a fatal brain tumor. As I was praying, in my spirit, I saw this black gob leave his head and I threw it to the floor. I knew it was gone and he knew it was gone. This was the gift of faith in action. About six months later I heard that he had died. I was devastated. I knew that the tumor was gone, and I knew what the Lord had done. My faith was shattered. How could I have been so deceived? About six months later I talked with his brother and told him about the brain tumor and how we had prayed for it. He said, "Oh, he didn't die from a brain tumor, that was gone. He died of something totally unrelated." Praise God for His gift of faith!

- "For all who are being *led* by the Spirit of God, these are the sons of God." Romans 8:14

We are to be led in our prayers by the Spirit of God not by our carnality. A carnal Christian is one that is led by his five physical senses. He is led by what he can touch, see, smell, hear or taste.

Note: There are times when you may be led to pray for a person who is not a believer. If you are being led by the Spirit of God, it makes no difference whether he believes or not. Where the Lord is working there is healing and wholeness. This may lead to a wonderful opportunity to lead that person to the Lord.

- "...and when they had come to Mysia, they were trying to go into Bithynia, and the Spirit of Jesus did not permit them:" Acts 16:7

Paul could have argued with the Lord and said. "You told us to go everywhere and preach the gospel." But instead they followed the Holy Spirit's leading, which this passage says is the Spirit of Jesus.

Jesus was led by the Father when Lazarus was sick.

- "When therefore He heard that he was sick, He stayed then two days longer in the place where He was," John 11:6

- Everything was pointing to the fact that he had better get there quick, but instead He waited on the Father.

• "And it came about one day that He was teaching; and there were some Pharisees and teachers of the law sitting there, who had come from every village of Galilee and Judea and from Jerusalem; *and the power of the Lord was present for Him to perform healing.*" Luke 5:17

• Jesus therefore answered and was saying to them, "Truly, truly, I say to you, the Son can do nothing of Himself, unless it is something He sees the Father doing; for whatever the Father does, these things the Son also does in like manner." John 5:19

Three times I have been directed not to pray for a particular persons healing. The Lord had something better in mind. But you can always pray for peace, patience, and trust. Do not be embarrassed to wait on the Lord and seek his guidance as you pray.

Note: There may be times when you are directed to pray for a person in a coma or who has brain damage. Remember, prayer is not a mental exercise but a spiritual leading of the Holy Spirit. Maybe their brain is dead, but their spirit is alive and well. Speak to their spirit.

Note: There was a young boy named Cameron, about two years old, who was brought to our Bible Study. He had received shaken baby syndrome when he was an infant. The doctors said he had no brain activity. His father is now in prison for a long time. I asked the foster parents, (who are Mormons) if I could pray for him, they consented and as I held him in my arms, I could feel the presence of the Lord was there to heal. His mind was gone, but his spirit was alive and well. As I prayed for him, he sat up and began smiling and rocking back and forth. Two years later I learned that he was walking with the aid of his parents. What a mighty God we serve.

- "Now faith is being sure of what we hope for and certain of what we do not see." Hebrews 11:1 Amplified Bible

Where did you get it?

- "And on the basis of faith in His name, it is the name of Jesus which has strengthened this man whom you see and know; and the *faith which comes through Him* has given him this perfect health in the presence of your all." Acts 3:16

It is not the activity that makes something good or bad, it is the origin of that activity. If it is directed by God, it is good. If it is not directed by God, no matter how good it seems, it can be bad.

Christians don't follow signs, signs follow Christians.

- "Jesus therefore said to them again, Peace be with you; as the *Father has sent Me, I also send you.*" John 20:21

Jesus walked by the power of the Holy Spirit, with total dependence on the Father. We are to walk by the power of the Holy Spirit, with total dependence on the Father.

- "As Thou didst send Me into the world, I also have sent them into the world." "I do not ask in behalf of these alone, but for those also who believe in Me through their word;" John 17:18-20

- "My sheep hear my voice, and I know them, and they follow Me;" John 10:27

Note: Are you trusting in the word or the One (Jesus) to whom the word is pointing?

Are you trusting in your prayers or the One (Jesus) to whom you are praying?

Are you trusting in the promises or the One (Jesus) who promised?

THE REAL FAITH

As the life of the flesh is in the blood, so faith is the life that flows into the roots.

A tree does not and cannot produce life. The tree is the carrier of the life flowing through its branches. The roots are not the life, they are the carrier that transports life into the tree. The roots can produce nothing without the life. The life is in the nourishment traveling to the roots to cause the tree to grow and produce fruit. The tree does not need to struggle or try to produce life, it cannot do it, only the life flowing through the tree can produce life. You are not the life, you are a carrier of the life produced by the one who said; "I am the way the truth and the life." Real Faith is the life that flows into the roots. The roots do not produce the life, but the life produces and nourishes the roots. It is the life that is flowing into the roots that is known as the real faith. You can never struggle or try hard enough to produce life. The life can only be produced by the One who is Life. "Jesus is the author and perfecter of our faith." (Hebrews 12:2)

Living water gives life; life giving water. "...but whoever drinks of the water that I shall give him shall never thirst; but the water that I shall give him shall become in him a well of water springing up to eternal life." John 4:14. Your mind cannot create life. Have we reduced faith to nothing more than an exercise in the metaphysical? Nowhere in the Bible does it tell you that you need to try harder.

If it were possible to attain faith for the task by our own struggling and trying to believe, then all glory would go to us. Have we substituted belief and trust for real faith? You say you believe, and that's fine but the devils also believe and tremble, James 2:19.

Faith is either a Fruit of the Spirit (Galatians 5:22) or a Gift of the Spirit (1 Cor.12:9). You know that; love, joy, peace, patience are all fruit of the Spirit given to us by grace through faith. Why do you struggle to have faith when it too is a gift given to us by grace through faith? The faith of God is imparted to man for the need of the moment.

Can you imagine a branch struggling and trying to produce life when out of its innermost being it flows naturally when needed? In Him is Life. You tell me you have faith, I would ask; "Where did you get it?"

Ephesians 6 tells us to; take up the full armor of God (His Armor), having girded your loins with truth, (His Truth). Put on the breastplate of Righteousness (His Righteousness) and having shod your feet with the preparation of the Gospel of Peace, (His Gospel, His Peace), in addition to all take up the Shield of Faith, (His Faith) and the Helmet of Salvation (His Salvation) and the sword of the Spirit (His Sword) which is the word of God. When you put on His Armor the enemy sees God.

Faith for salvation was given to you as a gift. Ephesians 2:8 "For by grace you have been saved through faith; and that not of yourselves, it is the gift of God."

"As you therefore have received Christ Jesus the Lord, (by grace through faith) so walk in Him (by grace through faith). Colossians 2:6 His Faith.

Heavenly Father; forgive me for struggling and trying to produce faith that can only come from you. You are the One who is working in us both to will and to do of Your good pleasure. You are the author and finisher of our faith. I trust You to be faithful to give us the faith we need for the need of the moment. Thank You for blessing us with Your presence and for allowing Jesus Christ to live His life through us. In Jesus Name, Amen.

LAYING ON OF HANDS

- "...they will lay hands on the sick, and they will recover." Mark 16:18

Note: In the Old Testament if the unclean touched the clean the clean would become unclean. If the clean touched the unclean the clean would become unclean. This is shown many times in Leviticus. In the New Testament when the clean, Jesus, touched the unclean, Lepers, the unclean became clean. Jesus did not become unclean. We are in Him and we will not become unclean when we touch the unclean.

In the New Testament the act of laying on of hands symbolizes the bestowal of blessings and benediction (Matt. 19:13,15 Luke 24:50) the restoration of health (Matt. 9:18 Acts 9:12,17) the reception of the Holy Spirit in baptism (Acts 8:17,19 19:6) the gifts and rights of an office (Acts 6:6, 13:3 1 Timothy 4:14 2nd. Timothy 1:6).

- "While He was saying these things to them, behold, there came a synagogue official, and bowed down before Him, saying, "My daughter has just died; but come and lay Your hand on her, and she will live." Matthew 9:18

- "And the Lord said to him, "arise and go to the street called Straight, and inquire at the house of Judas for a man from Tarsus named Saul, for behold, he is praying, and he has seen in a vision a man named Ananias come in and lay his hand on him, so that he might regain his sight." Acts 9:11-12

- "And Ananias departed and entered the house, and after laying his hands on him said, "Brother Saul, the Lord Jesus, who appeared to you on the road by which you were coming, has sent me so that you may regain your sight, and be filled with the Holy Spirit." Acts 9:17

I have found that through laying on of hands the person knows that you are praying for them personally. Sometimes, if you don't know the person well, you may want to ask them for permission to pray for them in this way. The Lord is compassionate and gentle, so should you be.

The Spirit of God is active in a believer and many times He is acting when we don't know it. Allow Him to work through you to touch others.

- "Do not lay hands upon any one too hastily and thus share responsibility for the sins of others; keep yourself free from sin." 1 Timothy 5:22

Note: To give an opposite illustration of the power of God working through a believer. I was walking into the San Diego Zoo years ago and a Hari Krishna missionary came up to me and attempted to put a smiley face on me. He got about two inches away and the Spirit of God threw him to the ground. I did not touch him, but the Holy Spirit did not want him touching me. 1 Timothy 6:20 says to guard what has been entrusted to you.

Laying on of hands for healing helps the sick person to release his faith, gives a personal point of contact and is usually associated with impartation of the Holy Spirit.

I had a young man in our Wednesday Prayer meeting who was being constantly attacked by the enemy. I knelt down by him to pray and I heard the enemy calmly say, "May I have permission to leave?" I calmly said, "Yes, you have permission to leave, in the Name of Jesus, never to return again." You don't have to make a big deal out of it drawing attention to yourself. Simply allow God to work in and through you.

CALL FOR THE ELDERS

Sometimes we all need a little boost in our faith, or a little something extra to help our faith. God in His goodness has provided a way.

- "Is anyone among you sick? Let him call for the elders of the church, and let them pray over him, anointing him with oil in the name of the Lord; and the prayer offered in faith will restore the one who is sick, and the Lord will raise him up, and if he has committed sins, they will be forgiven him." James 5:14-15

The believer is to call for the elders, deacons or whoever are men of faith in the local assembly. If none are available, the husband is considered the Priest and the head of the body of believers in his household.

Anointing oil is usually olive oil and it may have a little perfume in it. Oil in the scripture is usually a symbol of the Holy Spirit. Oil in the scriptures was also used as medicine to aid in healing of wounds. Anointing is always done with a purpose. David was anointed to be king. We anoint with the purpose of healing as we allow the Lord to bless others through us.

The prayer offered in faith (or the prayer of faith,) which was discussed earlier under the "gift of faith." Will restore, or save, the one who is sick.

Note: *As you can see, we can use our five physical senses to aid our faith. We can see the elders, we can smell the oil, we can feel the elder's hands, we can hear the elder's prayer and we can taste and see that the Lord is good.*

In 1978 I was a very good skier and we had a ski area about 8 miles from our house. I was skiing alone and coming down the mountain at a high rate of speed. I caught an edge and did a turn and a half in the air. I came down on my head and heard a loud bang. My poles, goggles and glasses were strewn about the hill like a yard sale. After gathering everything I skied down to my car. I knew I was hurt but I didn't know how bad it was. While driving home I could not hold my head up without propping my hand on my head while leaning against the door. When I got home, I laid down on the couch and asked my wife to call our Pastor to come to the house and pray over me. I could not get off the couch, I knew I had a potential broken neck. He came with our new youth pastor. After they prayed, I jumped off the couch and asked them if they wanted a cup of coffee. The Lord had healed my neck instantly. The place, on my body, where it was healed was so hot, I could not touch it. My wife felt it also and noticed how hot it was. This is just one instance of calling for the Elders of the Church.

We are blessed with pastors and elders that are open to prayer for the sick. If you need a little help with your faith, I'm sure your pastor and elders would be eager to pray with you.

ANOINTING OIL

Then Jesus came with them to a place called Gethsemane, Matthew 26 (Gethsemane means "oil press", He went to the place of the oil press in order to be crushed three times. To extract all the oil from an olive both the fruit and its' seed had to be crushed three times by a great weight in an olive press. The three crushing's in the Garden was a foreshadow of what was about to happen to Him in the physical.

The first crushing produced extra virgin olive oil and was used for light. The oil from the second press was used for medicine, while the oil from the third press was used for making soap for cleansing. In the Garden he went three times to be crushed.) and said to His disciples, "Sit here while I go over there and pray." And He took with Him Peter and the two sons of Zebedee, and began to be grieved and distressed. (Amplified; He began to show grief and distress of mind and was deeply depressed.) Then He said to them, "My soul is deeply grieved to the point of death; (Amplified; "My soul is very sad and deeply grieved, so that I am almost dying of sorrow." This was the start of the dying process.) remain here and keep watch with me." And He went a little beyond them, and fell on His face and prayed, saying. "My Father, if it is possible, let this cup (*God's wrath*) pass from Me; yet not as I will, but as Thou wilt." Luke 22:44 says: "And being in agony He was praying very fervently, and His sweat became like drops of blood, falling down upon the ground.

And He came to the disciples and found them sleeping, and said to Peter, "So, you men could not keep watch with Me for one hour? (Only He could bear our burdens, He had to bear the crushing alone). Keep watching and praying, that you may not enter into temptation; the spirit is willing, but the flesh is weak." He went away again a *second* time and prayed, saying, "My Father , if this cannot pass away unless I drink it, Thy will be done." Isaiah 53:4-5 "Surely our griefs (sickness) He Himself bore, and our sorrows, (pain) He carried; Yet we ourselves esteemed Him stricken, smitten of God, and afflicted. But He was pierced through for our transgressions, He was crushed for our iniquities; the chastening for our well-being (shalom) fell upon Him, and by His scourging we are healed." Isaiah 53:10,11 "But the Lord was pleased to crush Him, putting Him to grief; (made Him sick) if He would render Himself as a guilt offering, vs11 As a result of the anguish of His soul, He will see it and be satisfied, by His knowledge the righteous one. My servant will justify the many as He will bear their iniquities."

And He came back and found them sleeping, for their eyes were heavy.

And he left them again, and went away and prayed a *third* time, saying the same thing once more. This time for cleansing, (Isaiah 10:27 "So it will be in that day, that his burden will be removed from your shoulders and his yoke from your neck, and the yoke will be broken because of fatness. (The anointing oil)." Isaiah 58:6 "Is this not the fast which I chose, to loosen the bonds of wickedness, to undo the bands of the yoke, and to let the oppressed go free, and break every yoke?" Ezekiel 34:27 "Then they will know that I am the Lord, when I have broken the bars of their yoke and have delivered them from the hand of those who enslaved them." Galatians 5:1 "It was for freedom that Christ set us free; therefore keep standing firm and do not be subject again to a yoke of slavery." The yoke of the enemy is heavy – depression and oppression. Jesus said, "Take my yoke upon you, for my yoke is easy and my burden is light." Matthew 11:29-30

Then He came to the disciples, and said to them, "are you still sleeping and taking your rest? Behold, the hour is at hand and the Son of Man is being betrayed into the hands of sinners." It is now time for Him to experience physically what He just experienced spiritually. "Arise, let us be going; behold, the one who betrays Me is at hand!" Matthew 26: 30-46

Throughout the Old Testament anointing oil was used. In the New Testament Jesus became our anointing oil

Jesus came to be beaten, scourged and pierced for us, so that all that He is and all that He has will flow out into our life. His health, peace, abundance, favor, wholeness and life are all ours. He was crushed like the olive fruit to become our anointing oil. In the Old Testament when a lamb was brought to the priest the lamb was simply killed, not beaten up first. Jesus our lamb was beaten, scourged and pierced for us, by His stripes we are healed. Jesus dealt with the powers of darkness so we can be called "out of darkness into His marvelous light."

Jesus was thoroughly crushed so, in Him, we can be delivered from the power of darkness that attempts to crush us with sickness, mental oppression, and premature death. The anointing oil as well as communion is used to remind us of what Jesus did on the cross to provide everything we need so we can live in His wholeness in spirit, soul and body.

The "yoke" speaks of oppression that forces us to move in a certain direction. Addiction is a yoke that the enemy uses to pull you under and keep you where he wants you – defeated and unable to live the abundant life. You can see the chains of your addiction destroyed. Whether your addiction is to pills, drugs, alcohol, food, smoking, pornography or depressive thoughts, these yokes can all be broken as we count on His finished work on Calvary where He died for us.

1 John 2:20 "But you have an anointing from the Holy One," "The garment of praise for the spirit of heaviness" Isaiah 61:3

Acts 10:38 "You know of Jesus of Nazareth, how God anointed Him with the Holy Spirit and with power, and how He went about doing good and healing all who were oppressed by the devil, For God was with Him."

Luke 4:18 "The spirit of the Lord is upon me, because He anointed me to preach the gospel to the poor, He has sent me to proclaim release to the captives, and recovery of sight to the blind, to set free those who are downtrodden (oppressed). To proclaim the favorable year of the Lord."

DEALING WITH FEAR

The children of Israel could not enter the place of their promised inheritance due to unbelief (Hebrews 3:19) and disobedience (Hebrews 4: 4-11.) Fear produces unbelief and disobedience. Unbelief and disobedience produce fear.

The children of Israel who chose not to enter the place of their promised inheritance were still blessed by God for forty years as they wandered in the wilderness. He even blessed those ten spies who encouraged others to walk in unbelief and disobedience. Are we guilty of encouraging others to walk in unbelief and disobedience? God will still bless you because you are His, through the sacrifice of Jesus Christ.

As a Christian, If you walk in unbelief (Hebrews 3:19), (Hebrews 4:4 and 11) or disobedience, about certain truths in the Word of God, I don't care and what's worse, God doesn't care, He is not intimidated. God's Word is true whether we have been given the grace to believe it or not. There is no condemnation to those who are in Christ, God will not condemn or punish you if you don't believe. God will not force His way on anybody. God will not make you believe in anything, He will always give you a way out. He will not trap you into believing. He is a gentle shepherd, however if He has given you the grace to believe, He will honor that, If He has withheld His Grace, He will honor that also. You can't get mad at a blind person because he can't see. May we present all aspects of the gospel in such a way that men may choose to believe and trust God.

The biggest hindrance to our faith is fear.

Fear is doubting the love God has for us. If we knew and believed the love God has for us, we would never fear.

• "And we have come to know and have *believed the love* which God has for us, God is love, and the one who abides in love abides in God, and God abides in him. By this, love is perfected with us, that we may have confidence in the day of judgment; because as He is, so also are we in this world. There is no fear in love; but perfect love casts out fear, because fear involves punishment, and the one who fears is not perfected in love." 1 John 4:16-18

The enemy will do everything he can to make us doubt God's love. Fear is faith in evil. We have faith in God's love.

• "For I am convinced that neither death, nor life, nor angels, nor principalities, nor things present, nor things to come, nor powers, nor height, nor depth, nor any other created thing, shall be able to separate us from the love of God, which is in Christ Jesus our Lord." Romans 8:38-39

Let the enemy do his worst and we are still more than conquerors.

• "Even though I walk through the valley of the shadow of death, I *fear no evil*; for thou art with me;" Psalm 23:4

• "Surely goodness and mercy shall follow me all the days of my life; And I will dwell in the house of the Lord forever." Psalm 23:6 KJV

• "The Lord is my light and my salvation; Whom shall I fear? The Lord is the defense of my life; Whom shall I dread? When evildoers came upon me to devour my flesh, my adversaries and my enemies, they stumbled and fell. Though a host encamp against me, my heart will not fear; though war arise against me, in spite of this I shall be confident." Psalm 27:1-3

• "But he who listens to me shall live securely, and shall be at ease from the dread of evil." Proverbs 1:33

• "The Spirit of the Lord God is upon me, because the Lord has anointed me to bring good news to the afflicted; He has sent me to bind up the brokenhearted, to proclaim liberty to captives, and freedom to prisoners; To proclaim the favorable year of the Lord, and the day of vengeance of our God; to comfort all who mourn, to grant those who mourn in Zion, giving them a garland instead of ashes, the oil of gladness instead of mourning, the mantle of praise instead of a spirit of fainting. So they will be called oaks of righteousness, the planting of the Lord, that He may be glorified." (Quoted by Jesus in Luke 4:18). Isaiah 61:1-3

The enemy wants you to be afraid of evil. The purpose of terrorism is to make you afraid of evil and doubt God's love.

• "He will not fear evil tidings; His heart is steadfast, trusting in the Lord. His heart is upheld, he will not fear, until he looks with satisfaction on his adversaries." Psalm 112:7-8

• "When you lie down, you will not be afraid; when you lie down, your sleep will be sweet. Do not be afraid of sudden fear (*panic attacks*), nor of the onslaught of the wicked when it comes; for the Lord will be your confidence, and will keep your foot from being caught." Proverbs 3:24-26

If you're not safe in the lion's den with Jesus, then you're not safe anywhere.

• "For God hath not given us the spirit of fear; but of power, and of love, and of a sound mind." 2 Timothy 1:7 KJV

Thou shalt not sweat it. (paraphrased)

• "Blessed be the Lord, who daily bears our burden, the God who is our salvation. God is to us a *God of deliverances*;" Psalm 68: 19-20

Note: *When my wife is afraid, she will picture herself walking down the street with a lion on a leash.*

Nobody is going to try to harm you or try to bother you when you're walking with a lion. We have the lion of the tribe of Judah walking with us every day. Take the leash and start walking.

- I urge you to read and memorize Psalm 91. It will help to overcome fear.

- "The Lord will deliver me from every evil deed, and will bring me safely to His heavenly kingdom; to Him be the glory forever and ever. Amen." 2 Timothy 4:18

When going through a storm God will either calm the storm or God will calm His child.

- "The king of Israel, the Lord is in your midst; you will fear disaster (evil) no more." Zephaniah 3:15

Note: There are times when condemnation produces fear, shame, guilt, and a sense of unworthiness. We fear that we are not worthy due to some sin in the past, present or future. Condemnation is one of the primary tools of the enemy to oppress us. "Therefore there is now no condemnation for those who are in Christ Jesus. For the law of the Spirit of life in Christ Jesus has set you free from the law of sin and of death." Romans 8:1-2

In Christ it is okay to make a mistake. If you're going to make a mistake, make a mistake trusting God too much rather than too little. God will take you just as far as you allow Him.

REST IN HIM

The word *REST* holds with it the root of: calming of the winds. Calm and patient expectation. When you trust in the Lord the natural response is to rest in Him. Rest in What? There needs to be an object of our rest. This is explained in the following passage.

"There remains therefore a Sabbath rest for the people of God. For the one who has entered His rest has himself also rested from his works, as God did from His. Let us therefore be diligent to enter that rest, lest anyone fall through following the same example of disobedience." Hebrews 4: 9-11 (disobedience can be called a lack of appropriation, or unbelief.) If you want to struggle with something, struggle to enter His rest.

We cannot refuse to enter the Land of Promise, the place of our promised inheritance, due to our unbelief. "Let us therefore come boldly unto the throne of grace, that we may obtain mercy, and find grace to help in time of need." Hebrew 4:16 Our inheritance today is rest.

In the past, you may have struggled to believe the Lord for salvation, but once you were given the grace to trust His finished work, the struggle was over and the natural response was to trust in His finished work of salvation and rest in His love.

We have learned to destroy speculations and every lofty thing raised up against the knowledge of God, and we are taking every thought captive to the obedience of Christ. 1 Corinthians 10:5 We have learned that our life is hidden with Christ in God.

The word tells us, to rest in His:

Rest in His Protection: We learned that it was not our job to struggle to hang on to Him, instead we came to trust Him to hang on to us. He said; "I will never leave you or forsake you". "For it is God who is at work in you, both to will and to work for His good pleasure." Phil. 2:13 LET HIM! The Lord is faithful, and He will strengthen and protect you from the evil one." 2 Thess. 3:3 He showed Himself strong enough to bring you out of darkness, don't you think He's strong enough to keep you and protect you from the evil one? LET HIM! He is our strength and protector. - "…who are *protected by the power of God* through faith for a salvation ready to be revealed in the last time." 1 Peter 1:5 In Christ I am safe. I do not have to worry about myself. I am protected by the power of God. This boat can't sink with Jesus on board. Fear has no part in me. If I am not safe in the lion's den with Jesus, then I'm not safe anywhere. If I'm constantly concerned about protecting myself, I won't have time to be concerned for others.

Rest in His Redemption: A price had to be paid and He paid it. "He paid a debt that He did not owe because we owed a debt that we could not pay". I was saved, I am being saved and one of these days I will be saved. I have quit worrying about my salvation, it is a done deal. "Knowing that you were not redeemed with perishable things like silver or gold from your futile way of life inherited from your forefathers, but with precious blood, as of a lamb unblemished and spotless, the blood of Christ." 1 Peter 1:18 "For He delivered us from the domain of darkness, and transferred us to the kingdom of His beloved Son." Colossians 1:13

Rest in His Justification: I am Justified – Just as if I had never sinned. "Therefore, having been justified by faith, we have peace with God through our Lord Jesus Christ." Romans 5:1 I now have peace with God. I don't have to try to have peace with God. The Prince of Peace came to give peace with God. You won't experience the Peace *of* God until you realize we now have Peace *with* God.

Rest in His Sanctification: Regeneration. It is not me struggling and trying to live the Christian life. He never asked me to. He asked me to allow Him to live His life through me. It is surrender, as I allow Him to live His life through me. Not my *trying* but *trusting*. His obedience has become our obedience. Rom 5:19 Your obedience will give you confidence before God, not make you righteous. 1 John 2:28 1 Corinthians 1:2 "...to those sanctified in Christ Jesus and called to be holy,." 1 Corinthians 1:30 "But by His doing you are in Christ Jesus, who became to us wisdom from God, and righteousness and sanctification, and redemption." His sanctification has become our sanctification.

Rest in His deliverance from the Law: "There is therefore now no condemnation for those who are in Christ Jesus." Romans 8: 1 "Therefore my brethren, you also were made to die to the Law through the body of Christ, that you might be joined to another, to Him who was raised from the dead, that we might bear fruit for God." Romans 7:4 'But now we have been released from the Law, having died to that by which we were bound, so that we serve in newness of the Spirit and not in oldness of the letter." Rom 7:6 .- "knowing this, that our old self was crucified with Him, that our body of sin might be done away with, that we should no longer be slaves to sin." Romans 6:6 "Even so consider yourselves to be dead to sin, but alive to God in Christ Jesus." Romans 6:11

Rest in His Righteousness: "But to the one who does not work, but believes in Him who justifies the ungodly, his faith is reckoned as righteousness." Romans 4:5 "...and may be found in Him, not having a righteousness of my own derived from the law, but that which is through faith in Christ, the righteousness which comes from God on the basis of faith." Philippians 3:9

Rest in the fact that I am Forgiven: Colossians 2:13 "...He made us alive together with Him, having forgiven us all our transgressions."

Rest in knowing that, I have Eternal Life: "That whoever believes may in Him have eternal life. For God so loved the world, that He gave His only begotten Son, that whoever believes in Him should not perish, but have eternal life." John 3:15-16

Rest in knowing that, In Christ, I am Healed: "He himself bore our sins in His body on the cross, that we might die to sin and live to righteousness, for by His wounds you were healed." 1 Peter 2:24

Rest in His Provision: "And my God shall supply all your needs according to His riches in glory in Christ Jesus." Phil 4:19 *According to*, not *out of*. Abundantly beyond all you can ask or think. Is He the God of barely enough, just enough or more than enough?

This is just the beginning of what he has done for us. We have the down payment, there's more to come. May the Lord continue to bless you on the path that He has chosen for you, the path of resting in Him.

IN JESUS NAME

The Greek word for name is "onoma" and it means authority and character. To be sent or to speak in someone's name signifies to carry his authority and character.

Let's say one night you are sitting in your living room watching television and you hear a knock at the door. You turn off the television and you walk to the door and open it. Standing there is a uniformed officer who says; "I am here as the representative of the President of the United States. I would like for you to come with me." You would ask: "What authority do you have? Have you been authorized to use the Presidents name? Show me a letter of authority."

- "And when He had come into the temple, the chief priests and the elders of the people came to Him as He was teaching, and said, "By what authority are You doing these things, and who gave You this authority?" Matthew 21:23

When Jesus was tempted by the devil, the devil said to Him, "I will give You all this domain and its glory; for it has been handed over to me, and I give it to whomever I wish." Luke 4:6

The first Adam handed it over to Satan when he chose to disobey God. The Second Adam, Jesus Christ, came to restore that which was lost.

After His resurrection Jesus said. "All authority has been given to Me in heaven and on earth." Matthew 28:18

Note: *To pray in the name of Jesus is to pray as His representatives on earth, in His Spirit and with His aim in mind, and implies the closest union with Christ. Christians (Christ Ones) carry the name of Christ.*

• "Whatever you ask in my *name*, (authority and character) that will I do, that the Father may be glorified in the Son. If you ask me anything in my *name* (authority and character) I will do it." John 14:13-14

• "You did not choose me, but I chose you, and *appointed you*, that you should go and bear fruit, and that your fruit should remain, that whatever you ask of the Father in my *name*, (authority and character) He may give to you." John 15:16

• "If you shall ask the Father for anything, He will give it to you in my *name* Until now you have asked for nothing in my *name*; ask and you will receive, that your joy may be full." John 16:23-24

• "Therefore also God highly exalted Him, and bestowed on Him the *name* which is above every *name,* that at the *name* of Jesus every knee should bow, of those who are in heaven, and on earth, and under the earth, and that every tongue should confess that Jesus Christ is Lord, to the glory of God the Father." Philippians 2:9-11

• "And whatever you do in word or deed, do all in the *name* of the Lord Jesus, giving thanks through Him to God the Father." Colossians 3:17

As you can see praying in the name of Jesus is much more than tacking on a phrase at the end of a prayer. As we pray, we are using His authority and character, it's no wonder the enemy doesn't like it when we pray in Jesus name.

• "I pray that the eyes of your heart may be enlightened, so that you may know what is the hope of His calling, what are the riches of the glory of His inheritance in the saints, and what is the surpassing greatness of His power toward us who believe. These are in accordance with the working of the strength of His might which He brought about in Christ, when He raised Him from the dead, and seated Him at His right hand in the heavenly places, **far above all rule and authority and power and dominion, and every name that is named,** *not only in this age,* but also in the one to come." Ephesians 1: 18-21

• "But God, being rich in mercy, because of His great love with which He loved us, even when we were dead in our transgressions, made us alive together with Christ (by grace you have been saved), and *raised us up with Him,* and *seated us with Him in the heavenly places*, in Christ Jesus, in order that in the ages to come He might show the surpassing riches of His grace in kindness toward us in Christ Jesus." Ephesians 2: 4-7

There are times when we may be told, certain things are our positional standing not actual. These things may not become actual to you until we reckon or count them as true in our daily experience. As a good soldier for Christ.

Christians! Take your position!

SOME ADDITIONAL THOUGHTS

- "And raised us up with Him, and seated us with Him in the heavenly places, in Christ Jesus, in order that *in the ages to come* He might show the surpassing riches of His grace in kindness toward us in Christ Jesus." Ephesians 2:6

Note: Have you ever wondered what your loved ones who have died before you are doing? They are now living <u>in</u> the ages to come and the Lord is showing them the surpassing riches of His grace in kindness towards us in Christ Jesus. Can you imagine how many lifetimes it would take to enjoy the earth as we know it? Now can you imagine how long it would take to enjoy the universe? It would probably take an eternity. I don't think they are wasting their time looking down on us when they can experience the surpassing riches of His grace.

The poem on the following page expresses this thought:

David Bachoroski

I RECALL
By David Bachoroski

I recall the day He called you,
The day He called your name,
To be with Him in Glory,
No more to bear the pain.

Does He tell you that we miss you?
Does He tell you when we cry?
Does He cheer your heart with stories,
Of how we feel inside.

Is the pain now gone forever?
Each tear He's wiped away?
Have you seen the land of Canaan,
Is it everything they say?

Have you danced among the rainbows?
Have you skipped from star to star?
Do you every get discouraged,
And wonder where we are?

The time is growing near now,
Just a twinkle of an eye.
We'll meet you by the Gates of Pearl,
No more to wonder why!

- "Therefore everyone who hears these words of Mine, *and acts upon them*, may be compared to a wise man, who built his house upon the rock." Matthew 7:24

Note: If I pray for you and you are healed, tell me who has just received the gift of healing? You have! There are those in the Body of Christ who have the ministry of healing to administer the gift of healing to the body. The Lord is the one who heals, they are simply the minister of that gift.

Once God gives you something, He will not take it back. The enemy may try to steal it or tell you that you don't have it, but God is not going to take it back.

- Romans 11:29 says "...for the gifts and the calling of God are irrevocable."

- "Whatever you devise against the Lord, He will make a complete end of it. Distress will not rise up twice." Nahum 1:9

SAVE - in the Greek is the word sozo, — to save, i.e. deliver or protect - heal, preserve, save, do well, be made whole.

Frequently healing deals with time. Time is in the Lords hands and he can do instantly what may normally take a long time.

There are times that healing includes restoration: In Mark 3 The Lord saw a man with a withered hand, He said to the man, "Stretch out your hand." And he stretched it out, and his hand was *restored*. Also in Luke 22:50 the slave of the high priest, Malchus, had his right ear cut *off* by Peter when they came to arrest Jesus. He restored his ear.

- "He gave them authority over unclean spirits, to cast them out, and to heal every kind of disease and every kind of sickness." Matthew 10:1

Note: Jesus had to give them that authority at that time because the Holy Spirit was not yet given.

Note: Have you ever wondered, "Why is it that I can believe and pray for others and get results, but I find it difficult to believe and pray for myself?"

The answer may be found in 1st Corinthians 13:14-27. Every part of the body needs the other parts of the body. If you were able to do it alone, you wouldn't need the rest of the Body of Christ.

"Walk with the Healer, and you will be healed!"

I believe that too many times Christians are guilty of seeking all that God can give them instead of seeking God. When we have Him we have it all!

God Loves You.
May you be given the grace to trust Him.

This ends this part of our study.

"TESTING"

Careening down the mountain, smoke pouring out of the wheel wells, the sickening odor of burning brake pads filling your nostrils with a stench that can last for days. Your observer tells you that you're at a thousand degrees and the temperatures are rising. You're coming to the most hazardous part of the course, "Hairpin Turns". Keep your wits about you, don't let your mind wander, rely on the gauges and your experience. Watch the....

Testing – The very thought of the word can cause a tightness in the pit of your stomach. It can cause sweaty palms and your pulse rate to rise. The following are some of the truths concerning testing that I have learned through over 30 years of testing cars for the General Motors Proving Ground on Pikes Peak.

We put the vehicles components through an examination or trial to test its value. This is done to establish as true the components worth or character or to prove it. A test is an event that tries one's qualities. When the Lord gives you a quality such as Faith, Love, Joy, Peace, Patience, Goodness, i.e. the Fruit of the Spirit as in Galatians 5:22, He then proves that quality to establish it as true by experience or trial in your life.

A *test* is to prove to you what you have, not to prove it to others. A *trial* is to prove to others what God has given you.

The Lord will never test in your life what you do not have. We do not run a tire test with a spark plug, we run a tire test with a known good tire to prove or establish as true the value of that tire. God will only test what we have been given, not what we don't have. That is why when you pray for patience, the proof that you have that patience you prayed for is the test that follows. This proves to you that the Lord has heard your prayer and has enacted that quality in you.

When you received Jesus into your life you were given the Fruit of the Spirit. But they were not made real to you until you accepted them as part of your new life in Christ, and God proved to you that you have those qualities. He proved it, or established it as true in your daily experience by trials or tests.

I do not test cars because I hate cars, but instead it is because I love cars and want to make them better. God does not put us to the test because He hates us and wants to punish us, (Christ took our punishment for us), but instead because He loves us and wants us to live a victorious life by knowing what He has given us in Christ Jesus.

I hit the brake pedal for the last time, there was nothing left. I found the breaking point. I knew what we had to do to make the car better. We were coming to one of the hottest parts of the course with nothing left…

We test cars beyond the breaking point of everyday usage. Every part is tested to the extreme of operating conditions. A word of encouragement to you. God is faithful. 1 Cor. 10:13 says, "No temptation has overtaken you but such as is common to man; and God is faithful who will not allow you to be tempted beyond what you are able, but with the temptation will provide the way of escape. Also, that you may be able to endure it." God knows your breaking point and will not allow you to be tested beyond it. He knows just what He's doing. He created you and knows all about you. Testing is designed to build you up, not to tear you down.

Now we can better understand James 1:2-4 where He says, "Consider it all joy, my brethren, when you encounter various trials, knowing that the testing of your faith produces endurance. And let endurance have its perfect result, that you may be perfect and complete, lacking in nothing." And James 1:12 says, "Blessed is a man who perseveres under trial; for once he has been approved (passed the test) he will receive the Crown of Life, which the Lord has promised to those who love Him."

There was only one thing to do, let the brakes cool, they would re-cover if I could only let them cool, must allow them to cool. I dropped the transmission into low gear, there was some slowing but not enough. The hill was getting steeper, must stop the car. Finally, *the way of escape*, I came to a wide spot in the road and powered to a 180-degree spin. We were now going back up the hill, the brakes would now cool as we proceeded up the hill.

"You, who are protected by the power of God through faith for a salvation ready to be revealed in the last time. In this you greatly rejoice, even though now for a little while, *if necessary,* you have been distressed by various trials, that the proof of your faith, being more precious than gold which is perishable, even though tested by fire, may be found to result in praise

and glory and honor at the revelation of Jesus Christ."
1 Peter 1:5-7

I believe that the highest kind of praise that we can give to God is to *trust Him* when we are going through various tests and trials.

- 2 Corinthians 9:8 says "And God is able to make all grace abound to you, that always having all sufficiency in everything, you may have an abundance for every good deed."

So, as you can see a test is an event that tries one's qualities to prove or establish as true by experience or trial. The Lord is merely showing to you what He has already given you in Christ Jesus. Praise God for His willingness to share His life with us!

My observer was calmly taking the last of the test data and finishing his report, *he trusted me*. He smiled as I looked at him and said, *Thank You!*

Whenever talking about healing the topic of Paul's thorn in the flesh always comes up. The following is an exposition of this topic.

THORN IN THE FLESH

Proper exposition of God's word requires that scriptures should be read in context and explained in context.

- "And because of the surpassing greatness of the revelations, for this reason, to keep me from exalting myself there was given me a thorn in the flesh, a messenger of Satan to buffet me - to keep me from exalting myself! Concerning this I entreated the Lord three times that it might depart from me. And He has said to me, "My grace is sufficient for you, for power is perfected in weakness," most gladly, therefore, I will rather boast about my weaknesses, that the power of Christ may dwell in me." 2 Corinthians 12:7-9

- Right before that Paul was saying in 2 Corinthians 11:23-30.

- "Are they servants of Christ? (I speak as if insane) I more so; in far more labors, in far more imprisonments, beaten times without number, often in danger of death. Five times I received from the Jews thirty-nine lashes. Three times I was beaten with rods, once I was stoned, three times I was shipwrecked, a night and a day I have spent in the deep, I have been on frequent journeys, in dangers from rivers, dangers from robbers, dangers from my countrymen, dangers from the Gentiles, dangers in the city, dangers in the wilderness, dangers on the sea, dangers among false brethren; I have been in labor in hardship, through many sleepless nights, in hunger and thirst, often without food, in cold and exposure. Apart from such external things, there is the daily pressure upon me of concern for all the churches. Who is weak without my being weak? Who is led into sin without my intense concern? If I have to boast, I will boast of what pertains to my weakness."

Note: Would you say that Paul was buffeted, harassed, tormented and received constant opposition from the enemy. Paul's goal was to preach the gospel and everywhere he went he was opposed. This opposition was a messenger (angel) of Satan to buffet him.

The Greek word Aggelos was used 188 times in the New Testament. It was translated 181 times as angel and 7 times as messenger. Paul knew the Old Testament and often times used its terminology.

- "But if you do not drive out the inhabitants of the land from before you, then it shall come about that those whom you let remain of them will become as pricks in your eyes and as thorns in your sides, and they shall trouble you in the land in which you live." Numbers 33:55

- "Therefore I also said, I will not drive them out before you; but they shall become as *thorns in your sides*, and their gods shall be a snare to you." Judges 2:3

We don't use the term thorn today, but we do use the term pain in the neck.

Paul understood the authority of the believer and was given such revelations which a "man is not permitted to speak". 2 Corinthians 12:4 so to keep him from becoming too exalted (elated - in the Phillips translation.) he was given an angel of Satan to constantly buffet, torment and harass him. This was not given to him by God but it was allowed for a season.

He sought the Lord three time that this might depart from Him and the Lord said "My grace is sufficient for you, for my power is perfected in weakness. The Lord didn't tell Paul he had to live with it. He said that His grace is sufficient. Paul learned that the Lord's grace was sufficient in all things and in all circumstances and Paul learned how to overwhelmingly conquer through Jesus Christ.

- "But in all these things we overwhelmingly conquer through Him who loved us. For I am convinced that neither death, nor life, nor angels, nor principalities, nor things present, nor things to come, nor powers, nor height, nor depth, nor any other created thing, shall be able to separate us from the love of God, which is in Christ Jesus our Lord." Romans 8:37-39

Be careful that you do not base your doctrine on one passage taken out of context.

I will agree that Paul had some health problems, probably his eyes, I do not know for sure, but that is not what he was talking about in this passage.

You cannot use what you see in my body as a basis for your theology. Neither can you use what is happening to others in their body as a basis for your theology. Our theology needs to be based solely on God's Word. Does what is happening to me invalidate God's word? No! Neither does what is happening to others. If we base our theology on what we can see, touch, taste, hear or feel we are carnal.

• "But you followed my teaching, conduct, purpose, faith, patience, love, perseverance, persecutions, sufferings, such as happen to me at Antioch, at Iconium and at Lystra; what persecutions I endured, *and out of them all the Lord delivered me!* And indeed, all who desire to live godly in Christ Jesus will be persecuted." 2 Timothy 3: 10-12

ABOUT THE AUTHOR

David Bachoroski is retired from General Motors Corporation where he tested cars on Pikes Peak for 33 years. He is currently Chairman of the Pikes Peak Hill Climb Historical Association. an office that he has held for 10 years.

After thirty-three years of automobile testing with the General Motors Proving Ground, David retired in 1998. He was Manager of the GM Pikes Peak Vehicle Test Headquarters in Manitou Springs, Colorado and has completed over five thousand round trips to the Summit of Pikes Peak, touted as the world's highest highway at 14,110 feet.

David Bachoroski

Twelve times he was the Pikes Peak Hill Climb Pace Car Driver. He also built and prepared pace cars for such notables as Elke Summers, Rick Mears, Johnny Parsons, Sr., Al Unser, Jr. and Louis Unser. Ten times he was Pikes Peak Hill Climb car owner and builder with driver Jerry King, and assisted race crews with such notables as Bobby Unser, Sr., Robbie Unser, Bobby Unser,

Jr., Larry Ragland and brothers Frank and Nick Sanborn.

He also served two terms on the City of Colorado Springs Pikes Peak Highway Advisory Commission. He assisted Mankato State University with a Guiness World Record of first solar car to the Summit of Pikes Peak in 1990 and was founder and organizer of the 1992 Pikes Peak Solar/Electric Challenge, in which he worked with colleges and universities throughout the country.

He was nominated for Who's Who of Business Leaders in 1993 and was the subject of numerous articles in the Colorado Car Book, author Bud Wells, Race to the Clouds, author Stan Degeer, Denver Post, Rocky Mountain News, Gazette Telegraph and Pikes Peak Journal.

Bachoroski attended Adams State College in Alamosa, Colorado, where he majored in Business and music and has a Business Degree from Blair Business College, and an Automobile Mechanics Degree from Commercial Trades Institute.

He lives in Colorado Springs, CO, with his wife Connie, and has two daughters living near them, Stephanie and Michelle. Hobbies include, guitar playing, teaching and writing. He is also a member of the First Evangelical Free Church where he has held many offices since 1974. He and his wife became born again Christians in 1972. David went through a period of three years where he could read nothing but God's Word; no newspapers, magazines or television. He needed the cleansing power of God's Word up to twenty hours a day. He learned that; "you shall know the truth and the truth shall set you free." This could be called his personal Bible School. After that he has taught at numerous Bible Studies, and led many prayer groups for over 40 years, and has seen many lives changed.

BOOKS BY DAVID BACHOROSKI

The Glory of Man
by David Bachoroski

Glory. The very word is packed full of meaning. In the contemporary sense, we tend to think of it in terms of honor, distinction or esteem.

A nation's heroes are often its founders, who received wide acclaim due to their heroic efforts in battle, exploration, discovery, or courageous confrontations defying great odds. One thinks of Alexander the Great, George Washington, Lewis and Clarke, just to name a few.

In the sports world most would agree that many inspiring figures have received, or in some cases lost their glory.

The special distinction of glory extends to the arts, whether it concerns renowned paintings like DaVinci's, Mona Lisa, or grand statues such as Michelangelo's, David. It also includes varieties and styles of music, stage productions, literary masterpieces, poems, and supremely produced films. The point is, we know glory when we see it. What these incomplete lists illustrate is the glory we both see and ascribe to the people involved in talented and creative endeavors.

Yet there is more:

The Lord tells us in 1 Peter 1:24-25, "The glory of man is as the flower of grass. The grass withers and the flower falls off, but the Word of the Lord endures forever." In contrast the glory of God is absolutely true and changeless.

The true glory or worth of man is the ideal condition in which God created man. This ideal condition was lost in the fall, spiritual death, and is recovered through the work of Jesus Christ. In the final analysis, it is God's opinion alone that marks the true value of things as they appear to the eternal mind, and *God's favorable opinion is true glory, The Glory of Man.*

Dead Reckoning
By David Bachoroski

Why can't I do what is right? Many of us have asked this very question. We have tried to overcome our fleshly desires by self-determination, will power, joining focus groups, accountability groups, and 12 Step programs. David expounds on the power of Jesus to overcome addictions, thought patterns, and harmful habits in this short book, *Dead Reckoning.*

"Likewise reckon ye also yourselves to be dead indeed unto sin, but alive unto God through Jesus Christ our Lord." Romans 6:11

The only one who is capable of living the Christian life is Jesus Christ himself. He never asked us to lead this life by our own ability and by trying harder. He came to live his life *through* us. David shows how to overcome guilt, fear, condemnation, and how to appropriate the life of Christ in us, so that we may live the overcoming life God intended for us.

Healing and the Prayer of Faith
Third Edition
By David Bachoroski

In this foundational Bible study, David draws on both the Old and New Testaments with an emphasis on healing of spirit, soul, and body.

David shows God's desire to heal us through the finished work of the cross of Christ and the manifestation of the presence of God. This book is a faith-builder and provides a strong biblical basis for not just our own healing, but ministering healing to others. There are some who are not against healing, they are opposed to God doing it. All healing ultimately comes from God.

A way was provided in the Old Covenant for healing. It was conditional and based on the Law. The New Covenant of Grace is unconditional and demands that blessings are not earned but received by grace through faith in the finished work of the Lord Jesus Christ. Today we are under a better covenant. Our basis for healing cannot be based on the Law but on the Grace of God through the Blood of the Eternal Covenant.

Through this study we will better understand the ministry of praying for the sick according to the New Covenant. We desire to see the Divine Presence of God manifested in the local church and in His people as they are made whole in spirit, soul and body.

Some of the topics touched on are: Our relationship to the Law, The Covenants, Knowing God's Will, Doctors and medicine, Communion, The Gift of Faith, Laying on of Hands, Dealing with Fear, Resting in Him, Testing and Thorn in the Flesh.

Many of the deep things of God in scripture are not hidden from us they are hidden for us. To us that are being saved they are hidden in such a way that they may be found. When you hid your kids Easter eggs you hid them in such a way that they could be found. So it is with our loving Heavenly Father.

David Bachoroski came to the Lord in 1972 and for the past 40 plus years has been a Bible teacher in Colorado Springs, CO. His emphasis has been strengthening God's people through properly understanding the Word of God.

I trust this book will be a blessing to all who read it.

Flowing Streams Books
See our complete catalog and visit us online at
www.flowingstreamsbooks.com

www.ingramcontent.com/pod-product-compliance
Lightning Source LLC
Chambersburg PA
CBHW052013150726
47999CB00004B/1649